Walls of Words

How Boundaries Define Free Speech

by Thomas T. Taylor

Dear Esteemed Reader,

Thank you immensely for choosing this book to join your collection. We imagine that you've already embarked on an exploration of ideas within these pages, and we couldn't be happier about it!

Now, if you find yourself chuckling, pondering, or even debating with the words in front of you, we'd absolutely love to hear about it. If you can spare a few moments to pen down your thoughts in a review, we would be as delighted as a dictionary on a spelling bee!

An Amazon review would be excellent - but hey, we're far from picky. Whether it's a scribble on the back of a grocery list, a tweet, or even a message in a bottle (though that might take a while to reach us), your feedback is gold.

Writing a review might not be as fun as a spontaneous dance-off, but we promise it'll bring grins to our faces, warmth to our hearts, and incredibly valuable insights to future readers.

With Gratitude,

Bo Bennett, PhD
Publisher
Archieboy Holdings, LLC.

Table of Contents

Foreword:
A Brief Overview of the First Amendment

The intent behind this volume, "Walls of Words: How Boundaries Define Free Speech," is to provide a comprehensive exploration of freedom of speech in the United States, primarily focused on understanding the First Amendment. This foundational component of the American Bill of Rights is often cited but frequently misunderstood or misinterpreted.

Freedom of speech, as enshrined in the First Amendment, is held as an inalienable right, a vital cornerstone of a free state, and the backbone of Democratic society. Yet, its implementation, interpretation and enforcement is far from simple or homogenous, and it creates as many questions as it answers. That's where this book comes forth, intending to cast light on some of these complexities.

Our journey begins with an exploration into the rich landscape of speech in America, tracing the evolution and development of the First Amendment's implementation within our society. We delve into the minds and intentions of the founding fathers and how their vision continues to shape the interpretation of free speech today.

As we trace the path of jurisprudence, we'll explore landmark cases that left indelible marks on the First Amendment landscape, shaping and reshaping our understanding of what constitutes free speech. From the inkwell of the Supreme Court's bench to the dynamic arenas of public discourse, we look at how law and society interact to delineate the contours of free expression.

Of course, in a vibrant, ever-evolving democracy like ours, there's always a tussle between expression and restraint. We observe this vividly through the lens of media, perhaps the most potent tools of speech. An in-depth examination of media censorship, right from an era of early American media through the digital age, is provided. This journey provides enlightening insights into how the American approach to media freedom has evolved over time.

Important too is understanding when free speech transforms into a crime. This book explores the legal limitations to free speech, delving into the criminalization of certain forms of expressions. Incitement, obscenity, defamation, fraud, and harassment are just some of the key topics that we'll discuss in a bid to understand how the law draws the line.

Yet, it's not just the law that bounds our words, but societal norms and ethical considerations. The rise of disinformation, the blurred lines between satire and offensiveness, and the navigation of culturally sensitive speech are conundrums of the modern age that are both relevant and crucial conversation starters in our journey.

We will also investigate the ethical dilemmas associated with regulating speech and how personal and collective responsibilities could shape the future of free expression. We delve into the challenges of a rapidly evolving digital landscape, the ethical considerations of private censorship, and the international comparisons that shape our global conversation on free speech.

As we move forward, we assess the dynamic and somewhat precarious future of free speech. Technology's role in shaping our discourse along with the age old dichotomy between national security and personal freedom is dissected. Furthermore, we take a keen look at the critical role of education in maintaining the quality of informed expression in our society.

Finally, as collective gatekeepers of this crucial right, we conclude with a contemplation on our responsibilities. Having navigated the past and present landscapes of free speech in the US, we look ahead, projecting into the future. How must we adapt and evolve to ensure the continuance of this precious right in a landscape presenting new and unanticipated challenges?

This volume will equip you with the knowledge and perspective necessary to understand, cherish, and uphold the principles of free speech in an increasingly complicated and divided world.

Regardless of whether you're a student, legal professional, journalist, educator, or interested citizen, this book should cater to your intellectual curiosity and impart greater clarity on what the First Amendment actually means.

A comprehensive glossary of legal and media terms, along with summaries of landmark cases, has been included to ease comprehension. This invaluable guide should serve as a vigorous and clear-eyed alterative to conventional wisdom. It's the product of rigorous scholarship, intended for everyone who believes in the power of words and the necessity of their unimpeded expression.

We have tried to make this voyage as enlightening and engaging as possible, threading together legal principles, ethical debates, and cultural shifts that have and continue to mark the evolution of speech in America. It's an exploration not just of law, but of the heart of our democracy, our society, and our shared values and aspirations. Let's embark on this enlightening journey together.

Introduction: The Landscape of Speech in America

We inhabit a country that was founded on the principles of liberty and freedom, quite unparalleled in its fervent commitment to protect and invigorate the inalienable right to express oneself. In the American milieu, the sanctity of exercising free speech is enshrined in the First Amendment of our Constitution. This monumental legal document, paragon of the foundations on which our nation stands, guarantees this right almost without exception. However, the landscape of speech in America is more nuanced and layered than a glance at the Constitution would suggest.

As we delve deep into the matrix of American society, we discover that even something as ethereal and intangible as speech is bound by limitations. Boundaries of speech, you might wonder? It seems counterintuitive to the quintessential American mind trained to pride itself on free expression. Yet, it's true and vital to comprehend. These boundaries aren't an anomaly but a necessity; they are the vessels that contain the chaos, the madness, and the reckless abuses our freedoms otherwise could unleash.

Practically, today's America finds its speech bound by a multitude of factors: social norms, economic realities, political affiliicity, and cultural contexts. Free speech may be a constitutional right, but its application is often obscured by the tapestry of these dominant structures. Just as the lines we draw on a map demarcate territories and entities, so too do we draw boundaries in the realm of speech.

We're not just talking about overt regulations. It's also the more elusive, intangible boundaries defined by social norms and cultural values that guide our speech. These 'rules' can mark out what is acceptable and unacceptable dialogue within various societal domains, from a heated debate in a town meeting to a casual conversation at a country club.

There's also the vital understanding that free speech isn't always about the individual. On the contrary, it provides the scaffolding for constructive dialogues, catalyzes social changes, and nourishes our democracy. When a country eschews free discourse, it risks stagnation and an inevitably compromised future. It is within this vital need for dialogue that the landscape of speech takes on a profound importance.

Of course, there are inherent tensions in this portrayal of speech and its boundaries. Where does one person's freedom end, and another's begin? How does a nation balance the individual's right to express radically unpopular views with the community's potential revulsion and backlash? How do we foster a society where dissent is not suppressed but engaged with and acknowledged as a vital tenet within the marketplace of ideas?

And then there is the question of this elusive term we christen 'hate speech.' How does a society grapple with speech that seeks to systematically dehumanize or marginalize others based on their race, religion, or identity? Can we ever find a universally acceptable boundary for this, or will it forever be a subject of political and philosophical dispute?

What then of economic realities? Should the financially powerful have a louder voice than those struggling to make ends meet? Is it right that big corporations can use their financial clout to drown out the voices of the less fortunate? These are the economic boundaries that interplay with our developing discourse on free speech.

However, there is a beacon of hope in our increasingly polarized world, and that is the dynamism of our time. In every era, the shape and impact of free speech evolve, responding and adapting to the ever-changing landscape around it.

To understand the modern landscape of speech, we must place it within the context of historical struggles and triumphs. Each chapter of American history has shaped and been shaped by our evolving discourse on free speech. From the Civil Rights movement to the Free Speech movement of the 1960s and beyond, the past paints a vibrant backdrop against which we can understand our present.

Next, we must consider the rapidly expanding technological realities of our time. The influence of the digital age on the landscape of speech in America is immense. Social media platforms and the internet writ large have revolutionized how we communicate, opening up avenues for dialogue and exposing the wellsprings of our divided national psyche.

Another way to navigate this complex terrain is by examining the cases that have tested, challenged, and shaped our understanding of free speech in courtrooms. Each landmark case is a battle waged within the heart of America's ethos - a tug-of-war between interpretation, application, and the ebb and flow of societal norms.

Lastly, we cannot ignore the influence of our diverse cultural tapestry. American society is a complex amalgamation of multiple identities, belief systems, and perspectives. Our cultural fabric not only adds vibrancy to our discourse but also tests the elasticity of our understanding of free speech.

In conclusion, this book aims to take you on a journey through the contours of this complex landscape, exploring and defining the boundaries of free speech in America. It is written not to promote one viewpoint over another, but to engage readers in a deeper understanding of what it truly means to have the right to express ourselves freely in a diverse and evolving society. So let's set out to explore these 'Walls of Words' with a spirit of open inquiry, respect for varied opinions, and a commitment to advancing our collective understanding of this most pivotal right.

Chapter 1:
The First Amendment:
An In-depth Look

The First Amendment to the United States Constitution, a fundamental element of what we deem as the 'American freedom', is a complex concept with a vital role in defining our rights. At its core, the First Amendment safeguard our right to express, believe, and assemble. These freedoms, bestowed upon every American, make up the cornerstone of our country's democratic dispensation.

For many, the freedom of speech, protected under the First Amendment, is seen as synonymous with their American identity. However, the understanding of this right can often be a matter of personal interpretation. Some view the First Amendment as a carte blanche for all forms of speech - regardless of intention or impact. Unsurprisingly, this perspective tends to stir controversy and debate in our society. Yet, on the other end of the spectrum, there's an understanding that although speech is fundamentally free, it should not be devoid of responsibility, ethics, and respect for the rights of others.

In the subsequent chapters, we will dig deeper into the legal intricacies that make up the First Amendment. We will look at how court rulings throughout history have shaped its interpretation, how free speech pertains to social media, and the role of censorship in both protecting and limiting our rights. It's essential that we tread through the complexity of these legal constructs with an open mind, acknowledging that this fundamental American right is far more nuanced than what meets the eye.

Situated in the realm of constitutional law, the First Amendment, does not just guarantee the freedom of speech, but it prevents

Congress from making any law "respecting an establishment of religion, or prohibiting the free exercise thereof;" or "abridging the freedom of speech, or of the press; or the right of the people peaceably to assemble, and to petition the Government for a redress of grievances." Each of these provisions of this unique Amendment will be addressed in the subsequent chapters. The objective here is not merely to understand its legal language but to comprehend its grandeur, its impact on our society and its influence on the world.

The interpretation of the First Amendment has never been constant. It has evolved with each court ruling, responding to societal changes, technological advancements, and shifts in cultural values. At its heart, the First Amendment serves to instill a sense of freedom – a freedom to express one's views without the fear of governmental reprisal. Remember, this is also a freedom that bears its own set of boundaries. This book aspires to inform, educate, and stimulate discussions about this essential facet of American democracy.

The Founding Fathers' Intent

The Founding Fathers of the United States, formidable figures whose ideals shaped a nation, held free speech as a cornerstone of democracy. It was recognized as a collective reflection of society, a tool to challenge authority and a means to protect the minority from dictatorial majorities.

Often, people view the First Amendment as a catch-all protection clause against any form of limitation on speech. However, it's essential to remember that the Founding Fathers were not absolutists. They, too, acknowledged that a balance must be struck between the individual's right to free speech and the need to maintain societal health.

Take for example the famous incident in 1798 when the Federalist-controlled Congress passed the Alien and Sedition Acts. These laws prohibited public opposition to the government and were used to arrest and convict 10 Republican newspaper owners who criticized the federal government. This substantiates that even the contemporaries of the Founding Fathers found certain circumstances that warranted control over abstract liberties.

Yet perhaps the most telling interpretation of the Founding Fathers' intent can be gleaned from debating the Constitution's drafting. They infused the First Amendment with the democratic spirit, aiming to balance the government's authority with citizens' rights.

For instance, Thomas Jefferson's thoughts on free speech were recorded in his letter to James Madison in 1787. He wrote: "A Bill of Rights is what the people are entitled to against every government, and what no just government should refuse, or rest on inference." Jefferson believed the power to limit speech should never belong solely to the government, but that society should self-regulate to a certain extent.

The free press also commanded a vital place among the Founding Fathers' beliefs. They saw the press as the mouthpiece of the public, a platform to hold the government accountable. Benjamin Franklin, a printer himself, embraced this conviction. His writings expressed a belief in the necessity of the free press for the survival of a flourishing and informed democracy.

Amid these views, it's clear that the Founding Fathers were aware of speech's inherent potential for harm. They acknowledged that the right to free expression brought with it the responsibility to exercise that right thoughtfully and deliberately.

However, it's important to clearly state that they didn't intend free speech to be a platform for hate, discrimination, or violence. Their dedication to debating ideas, not individuals, was evident. They sought meaningful and constructive discourse.

Reflecting on the Founding Fathers' intent, it's clear they did not anticipate a world shaped by technological evolution. They crafted the First Amendment based on the times they lived in and the challenges they faced. Therefore, their intent should not be taken as an infallible guide to navigate the complex world of modern free speech.

Ultimately, the spirit of the First Amendment rests on engagement, respect, and balance. The Founding Fathers understood that free speech was a double-edged sword. Hence they intended it to cut through societal hypocrisies, not to wound fellow citizens.

With technological advancements continuously reshaping the discourse landscape, it's crucial that the essence and spirit of the Founding Fathers' intent be upheld. That means striking a delicate balance between fostering constructive debate and preventing harm.

The legacy of the Founding Fathers' intent is an ongoing commitment to democracy. It's a belief in free speech as a tool of change, a beacon guiding the majority while protecting the minority. Their wisdom should remain at the core of our discourse, deeply ingrained in our collective consciousness.

Indeed, by honoring the Founding Fathers' intentions, we not only recognize the importance of free speech but also the critical role of respect and understanding. The delicate dance of democracy, after all, is not about shouting the loudest, but about listening the most.

Understanding the complexity of the Founding Fathers' intent is fundamental in our ongoing dialogue on what free speech really means. We must strive to find that same balance that our Founding Fathers envisioned to ensure that free speech continues to promote positive discourse, peaceful protest, and change in our time and beyond.

The Evolution of First Amendment Jurisprudence

Originally implemented as a simple and concise principle, "Congress shall make no law... abridging the freedom of speech," the understanding and application of the First Amendment has come a long way over two centuries. Its interpretation has sculpted and been sculpted by the heartbeats of various eras, making it a living, evolving pillar of American jurisprudence.

Interestingly, the Supreme Court didn't really start to delve into free speech cases until late in the 19th century, marking the onset of First Amendment jurisprudence's formal evolution. In the seminal case, *Schenck v. United States* in 1919, Justice Holmes articulated the "clear and present danger" test for the first time, suggesting that this freedom wasn't absolute if it posed imminent peril.

Subsequently, the early part of the 20th century saw First Amendment doctrine dominated by a desire to balance citizens' freedom of expression against the government's need to maintain order and security, paving the way for cases such as *Gitlow v. New York* in 1925. Here, a state law prohibiting anarchy was upheld while also incorporating the free speech clause to apply to state laws as well.

Indeed, the jurisprudence around the First Amendment isn't a steady, progressive waltz towards greater liberties. The paradigm has often shifted with the political tides. This is especially visible during The Cold War era when (in a 1951 case, *Dennis v. United States*), the Court upheld the convictions of Communist party leaders for conspiring to advocate the violent overthrow of the government, embodying a certain hardening of the state against dissent.

Nevertheless, the pendulum swung back towards a more liberal interpretation with the dawning of the 1960s. It was in this flowering of civil rights and social revolution that a broadening of free speech protections was initiated. New standards and doctrines entered the picture, transforming how we understand First Amendment protections today.

This move towards a liberal interpretation is epitomized in the iconic case of *New York Times Co. v. Sullivan* in 1964. Here, the Court set a new standard for what constituted 'libel' against public officials, promoting a freer, more critical press. The ruling affirmed the necessity of "breathing space" for free speech and robust public debate.

Following the Sullivan verdict, the Supreme Court provided more structural form to the First Amendment with the *Miller test* in 1973, deciding what could be deemed 'obscene.' Similarly, the development of the 'viewpoint neutrality' principle and the 'forum analysis' test evidenced an ongoing evolution in the Court's First Amendment jurisprudence. These landmark decisions removed arbitrary subjectivity, making the adjudication on freedom of speech more consistent and predictable.

However, the First Amendment evolution is far from complete. The digital age brings with it new challenges, with a borderless internet often clashing with national laws. In recent years, the Supreme Court has grappled with how the First Amendment applies in cyberspace, resulting in cases like *Reno v. American Civil Liberties Union* in 1997 where the Court applied traditional free speech protections to the internet.

While technology continues to evolve at an almost bewildering pace, it's clear that the core principle of the First Amendment – the right to express oneself without fear of government retaliation or censorship – remains steadfast. It's this principle that the Supreme Court continues to wrestle with, striving to strike a fair balance between liberty and security, public order and personal freedom.

Beyond landmark cases and doctrinal shifts, it's insightful to note the influence of individual justices in shaping First Amendment jurisprudence. Figures such as Justice Hugo Black, with his 'absolutist' view of free speech, and Justice Oliver Wendell Holmes, known for his 'clear and present danger' test, have left indelible marks on the interpretation of the First Amendment. Their legacy continues to resonate in hearings even today.

Indeed, the trajectory of First Amendment jurisprudence shows us that free speech isn't a static concept. It adapts and grows with our society, reflecting the prevalent attitudes, fears, and aspirations of the nation. It's a journey that reflects the ebb and flow of the

American socio-political climate and its complex relationship with individual freedoms.

At its core, the First Amendment exists to prevent the government from restraining our thoughts and words. But with evolving contexts and threats, its jurisprudence has had to adapt. It's a constant negotiation between the extension of rights and the imposition of responsibilities, the protection of personal liberty and the preservation of public order.

In the end, the journey through the evolution of First Amendment jurisprudence is a testament to this fundamental truth: that free speech is an organic, living principle. Like the nation it serves, it's not rigid but flexible, mutable, and open to reinterpretation. This journey tells us that free speech, while foundational, is not finished. It's an ongoing evolution towards a greater understanding of our rights, responsibilities, and the contours of human liberty.

Major Landmark Cases

As we delve into the history of free speech in America, it is essential to highlight some major landmark cases. These cases have shaped the way we interpret and understand the concept of free speech. Their significance cannot be overstated as they have, in many ways, designed the landscape of discourse and expression in this country.

The 1919 case, Schenck v. United States, is perhaps one of the most significant in defining the limits of free speech. In this instance, Charles Schenck, a member of the Socialist Party, was charged with distributing pamphlets that allegedly obstructed recruiting during World War I. The ruling was a lesson in the balance of free speech and national security, shedding light on instances where societal safety and wellbeing can outweigh the right to free expression.

Brandenburg v. Ohio, a 1969 case, further shaped free speech jurisprudence by defining the scope of inflammatory speech that could potentially incite violence or harm. The U.S. Supreme Court defended a Ku Klux Klan leader's right to make a controversial speech, so long as it didn't incite imminent lawless action. It's a difficult line to draw, but one that enables both uncompromising dialogue and societal peace.

Near v. Minnesota (1931) is another landmark case in which the U.S. Supreme Court ruled against "prior restraint," which is the censorship of a publication before it is distributed. The ruling emphasized the public's right to access controversial points of view, to think, debate, and decide for themselves without government intervention - an essential defence against censorship.

It would be remiss not to mention the impactful case of New York Times v. Sullivan (1964). This case influenced modern libel laws and reinforced the importance of free press. In this lawsuit, a police commissioner sued New York Times for publishing an ad that he claim contained inaccuracies about him. The ruling emphasized the need to protect even erroneous speech in public discourse to ensure a free and robust debate.

Expressing opinions, even in the realm of education, came under examination in the Tinker v. Des Moines Independent Community School District (1969). The Supreme Court held that students' rights to free speech extended to public schools, demonstrating the reach of the First Amendment's power. This upheld the diverse perspectives and democratic principles in our educational institutions.

The case of Cohen v. California in 1971 broke new ground in the nebulous territory of offensive speech. The Supreme Court supported Cohen's right to communicate his dissatisfaction with the Vietnam War through his chosen attire, viz., a jacket bearing an explicit statement. This point emphasized that words themselves, regardless of taste or decency, are protected under free speech rights.

The Communications Decency Act's constitutionality came into question in the 1997 case of Reno v. ACLU. The court ruled against government efforts at online censorship, establishing a crucial precedent for speech rights on the internet and setting the stage for the vibrant digital speech we see today.

In the context of campaign finance, the Citizens United v. Federal Election Commission case from 2010 allowed corporations to use their treasury funds for political expenditures. The Supreme Court concluded that political spending is a form of protected speech, a ruling that significantly altered the landscape of American politics.

The Supreme Court's decision in 2010, in the Snyder v. Phelps case, was highly controversial. The Court ruled that offensive speech, in this case, by members of the Westboro Baptist Church at the funeral of a U.S. Marine, was constitutionally protected. Despite the emotional harm it caused, the court deemed the church's speech to be of public concern at the very core of the First Amendment's protection.

However contentious, the significance of the precedent set in each of these cases, alongside their rulings, cannot be denied. They serve as guideposts in interpreting the First Amendment with the expansive remit of free speech, testing its limits, and exploring its role in sustaining our democracy. Unsurprisingly, these decisions elicit fervent debates that touch on critical issues such as the nature of democracy, the limits of power, and the potential for societal harm.

When examining these landmark cases, it's important to consider not only the rulings themselves but also their impact on subsequent litigation and policy. In some cases, the interpretation of the First Amendment has been progressively broadened, while in others, it has been restricted, often due to conflicting societal interests or changing societal norms.

Despite the controversies these cases often fuel, they underline the fact that the interpretation of free speech is not set in stone. Instead, it evolves with society's needs and values, reflecting an adaptive legal system capable of dealing with technological advancements, political changes, and societal shifts.

As we continue the journey through this book, the exploration of these cases will provide us with a foundation to further understand the complexities of free speech. We'll see how these rulings, situated at the intersection of law and society, have challenged concepts, stirred debate, and, most importantly, protected the quintessentially American right to free speech.

Chapter 2:
Censorship in Media:
A Historical Perspective

The saga of censorship in American media is a historically complex and challenging one, fraught with battles over the very nature of free speech. Tracing its roots back to the early origins of our nation, we find stark contrasts between once prevailing societal norms and the relentless evolution of modern values. Much of what we may perceive as utterances of free will weren't so freely observed throughout history. The Sedition Act of 1798, for instance, was one of the first legal instruments used to suppress oppositional voices, back when our republic was in its infancy. It epitomized the ideological rift between the early defenders of unrestricted speech and those who prioritized national security over individual liberties. As media platforms proliferated from the printed press to radio, to television and the internet, so did the mechanisms of censorship. Broadcasters during the world wars were often met with explicit instructions about what they could and couldn't say on air. Media, often painted as the Fourth Estate and a bastion of free speech, has, for a substantial part of its history, navigated choppy waters of government oversight, societal pressures, and self-censorship. From battling acts like the Communications Decency Act in 1996, to the outcries over net neutrality in this digital age, the journey illustrates how the media has been in constant negotiation with the powers that be, continuously shaping and reshaping our understanding of what is deemed acceptable speech and what isn't. The narrative of a free press, it seems, is an ever-evolving one, artfully straddling the fine line between liberty and legality, weaving the tapestry of America's complex relationship with free speech.

The Beginnings: Early American Media and Censorship

The founding of the United States marked a significant turning point in history, signaling the advent of a new nation built upon principles of liberty and the pursuit of happiness. One of these foundational tenets centered on the issue of free speech - the right to express oneself openly without fear of retribution or censorship. In this formative stage, the country's early media played a critical role in shaping American thinking and in establishing guidelines for expression and censorship.

It's essential to remember that early American media took root in a time when the concepts of free expression and press freedom were still foreign to many. The First Amendment to the U.S. Constitution, ratified in 1791, formulates these rights: "Congress shall make no law...abridging the freedom of speech, or of the press." This was a radical departure from European norms where rulers severely restricted or controlled publishing and expression.

Unsurprisingly, the government didn't universally apply this principle in its early years. In truth, the U.S. government and other powerful entities often sought to suppress dissenting views. The Alien and Sedition Acts of 1798, for example, criminalized "false, scandalous, and malicious writing" against the government. This legislation clearly overstepped the boundaries of constitutional protection and marked an early instance of American censorship.

Yet, parallel to instances of censorship, the power of the press grew. Common individuals began to have their voices heard through pamphlets, newspapers, books, and even cartoons. Viewpoints varied widely from Federalist papers advocating for a robust national government to Thomas Paine's revolutionary pamphlet, "Common Sense". This explosion of free expression facilitated the development of diverse thought and democratic deliberation.

We can't gloss over the significant influence of Benjamin Franklin, arguably one of the most important figures in early American media. Franklin, a talented printer, writer, and publisher, was a steadfast advocate of free speech. His Pennsylvania Gazette was instrumental in pushing forward the discussion on civil liberties and government. His endeavor demonstrated the power of media in shaping public discourse, even as he danced around sensitive topics and potential censorship.

Throughout the 19th century, advancements in technology, such as the telegraph and photograph, revolutionized media, and communication. This innovation led to a greater dissemination of information, thereby further democratizing media access. Newspapers started evolving from partisan platforms to become more objective establishments committed to reporting the news with accuracy and balance.

But along with these advances, deleterious attempts to curb free speech also evolved. The Comstock Law of 1873 was a notable example of this trend. This law made it illegal to send obscene, lewd, or lascivious books through the mail. More severely, it had a chilling effect on a range of literary and medical publications, stifling open discussion on many topics seen as controversial at the time.

The early 20th century saw more tension between media and censorship. World War I and II spawned an atmosphere of fervent patriotism. The Sedition Act of 1918 and the Smith Act of 1940—both wartime measures—curtailed free speech under the guise of protecting national security. These Acts led to significant suppression of dissenting voices, particularly those against war, causing some of the darkest days for American free speech.

Yet in this same turbulent period, courageous pioneers in journalism relentlessly pushed back against censorship, striving to hold those in power accountable. The muckraker journalists, for example, sought to expose societal ills through investigative reporting, often facing threats and reprisals.

Jumping forward to the 1960s and 1970s, the U.S. found itself tangled in the Vietnam War and the Civil Rights Movement—both events posed serious challenges to the concept of free speech. The press played a dual role, inspiring essential conversations about liberty and justice while also facing censure and censorship from governmental and social factions.

When we reflect on the early history of American media and censorship, despite the numerous instances of attempted suppression, we see continued growth in the voice of the people. The spirit of openness, democracy, and dialogue was persistent. American society, powered by the audacity and resilience of journalists and ordinary individuals, kept pressing forward, proving that free speech is not just a constitutional right—it's also an enduring American ideal.

Let's also remind ourselves that these are not relics of history, but living, breathing narratives that are continuously evolving in America. As media and technology continue to transform rapidly in the digital age, the perimeters of free speech and the potential for censorship are being constantly reshaped and challenged in ways that early Americans could hardly have envisioned.

But even amid challenges and transformations, the commitment to protection of free speech remains an unwavering cornerstone of American democracy. It's what allows democracy to thrive and to keep the powerful in check. And it's our responsibility—as beneficiaries of the fights of the past—to ensure that this crucial freedom is preserved and deepened for future generations.

The Hays Code and Hollywood: Censorship on the Silver Screen

The ripple of effects that censorship has had on the arts — literature, music, and film — is somewhat astonishing. Perhaps most significant is the impact on Hollywood, and indeed, the concept of 'free speech' itself. In 1930, a pivotal moment in the history of American cinema unfolded: the introduction of the Hays Code, a set of morally-focused censorship guidelines, designed to dictate the narrative content of Hollywood films.

Spearheaded by Will H. Hays, the Code was adopted as a way for the film industry to regulate itself, rather than being regulated by external government bodies or censors. It provided a rigorous moral framework, prohibiting specific content such as nudity, profanity, and even ridicule of the clergy. In essence, the Hays Code was the epitome of self-censorship, and its effects were profound and far-reaching.

Narrative arcs were straightjacketed, crucial societal issues were glossed over, and depictions of reality were sanitized. Filmgoers were served a careful diet of narratives that embodied a specific traditional moral cosmos. It might not be immediately apparent, but this had profound implications for the concept of 'free speech' in American film, and society as a whole.

The argument was that these guidelines preserved moral order and adhered to a majority consensus of what was 'appropriate' for public consumption. Yet, it became evident that this was more about control and fear of the social implications of outright, unregulated expression. The very essence of free speech, the right to express without fear of penalty, was stymied under these regulations.

Indeed, free speech, by definition, ensures citizens the right to communicate their opinions and ideas without fear of government retaliation or censorship. However, the Hays Code exemplified a subtle, nuanced form of censorship under the auspices of moral guidance and self-regulation. This undoubtedly distorted the tenets of free speech.

So what happened? Real conversations were stifled. Instead of artists using the medium of film to grapple with complex societal issues, offer diverse perspectives, or challenge harmful norms, they were significantly limited in what they could depict.

However, resistance to the Hays Code began brewing towards the late 1950s, as societal attitudes shifted and the American public craved more realistic, gritty cinema. The reins of censorship began to loosen. By 1968, the Hays Code was replaced with the modern

MPAA film rating system, reflecting a significant societal shift towards open dialogue and explicit content — marking a notable victory for free speech.

Yet, the legacy of the Hays Code cannot be underestimated. It suggests the tensions between free speech and the intent to protect societal values can lead to a complex dance where the lines are blurred, and sometimes, deliberately obscured. This has shaped the industry's attitudes towards censorship and self-regulation in the United States and beyond.

It must be noted that the code's existence treads on precarious ground when it comes to the First Amendment. Was there a violation of the right to freedom of speech? While arguments can be made from both sides, the crucial aspect lies in the way this self-imposed censorship shaped, moderated, and edited the world's perception of American culture, along with the perception Americans had about themselves.

Swaths of the American populace were under-represented or completely invisible in mainstream Hollywood narratives. This distortion in representation is a concern, not least because it implies censorship of a different kind: the suppression of diverse experiences in favor of a homogenous, arguably sanitized, portrayal of American identities and lives.

As we look back at this slice of cinematic history, it forces us to question and consider the delicate balance of promoting creative freedom and the right to expression, against safeguarding social thought and moral preservation. The lessons learned from the Hays Code are not confined to the parameters of the film reel; they echo loudly within the larger conversation surrounding free speech.

We need to understand these murky waters of censorship in all forms, be it overt or self-imposed. The paradoxical idea of 'freedom through censorship' as expounded by the Hays Code, though inherently problematic, sparked vital debates around what true freedom of expression means, both within and beyond the silver screen.

Understanding the circumstances that gave rise to the Hays Code, the era it represented, and its eventual fall can provide great insights into the evolving boundaries of free speech. What is evident, though, is these instances of repression often catalyze the push for progress, nuance, and diversity in expression.

In conclusion, as we navigate the nebulous terrains of free speech, we are reminded of the need for discernment, dialogue, and a constant recalibration of our collective moral compass. The Hays Code underscores the far-reaching influence of censorship, illuminates the stark power dynamics at play, and gives us a sharper perspective on the vital question: how do we truly define free speech?

The Fairness Doctrine: Balancing Act on the Airwaves

Our discussion until now has explored the intricacies of where free speech begins and where it ends. Now, let's delve into a landmark policy from the annals of American broadcasting history: the Fairness Doctrine. Understanding this doctrine provides an important context in the greater discourse of free speech and strikes a reverberating chord even in today's climate.

The Fairness Doctrine, a policy introduced by the Federal Communications Commission (FCC) in 1949, was a regulatory measure aimed at maintaining a balanced, honest depiction of contrasting viewpoints on contentious issues over the public airwaves. The policy encompassed two primary principles: broadcasters were required to devote some airtime to discussing controversial matters of public interest, and they were expected to allow opposing views on such issues.

At its essence, the Fairness Doctrine was a governmental effort to ensure a democratic use of the public airwaves. Its main objective was to prevent any single interest group from monopolizing the discourse on controversial issues. It was a guiding principle for broadcasters, reminding them that they acted as stewards of the airwaves, which were a public resource.

But how was such a doctrine enacted, and more importantly, managed? In practice, the FCC used the Fairness Doctrine to guide rulings when complaints were lodged against a broadcaster. It's significant to note that the doctrine didn't advocate a strict time-allocation formula for differing views. Rather, it aimed for substantive coverage of diverse perspectives.

The Fairness Doctrine represented a significant recognition that the media act as gatekeepers of information and have a vital role to play in serving public interest. Indeed, the doctrine proposed that when a station broadcasts one point of view, it has an obligation to present contrasting views as well.

However, not all embraced the Fairness Doctrine as a champion of democratic discourse. Critiques of the doctrine emerged from two main camps. Some media experts and broadcasters felt the doctrine actually limited free speech by discouraging broadcasters from presenting controversial themes, fearing they may be required to provide time for opposing views.

In contrast, other critics worried that the doctrine didn't go far enough in promoting diverse voices. They argued that the ruling was challenging to enforce and often ignored, leading to a significant imbalance in the presentation of viewpoints, thereby narrowing the spectrum of discourse.

It's these debates that eventually led to the demise of the Fairness Doctrine in 1987. The FCC abolished the policy after concluding that it may actually inhibit the broader principle of free speech that it was intended to safeguard.

Post-abolition, there has been a significant shift in the landscape of broadcast media. Talk radio, for example, has burgeoned in the decades since the doctrine's demise. Critics claim that the decline of the doctrine has contributed to a rise in hyper-partisan talk shows and undermined the ideal of balanced, fair journalism.

Whether you hold the perspective that the Fairness Doctrine was a stalwart defender of democratic discourse or a restrictive barrier to free speech in the broadcast world, it's unarguable that it played a significant role in shaping public dialogue via the airwaves.

In retrospect, the doctrine underscores the inherent struggle to balance free speech with equitable representation. It also underlies the persistent challenge faced by regulatory bodies: how to guide the gatekeepers of information to serve the broadest public interest and promote a healthy democratic discourse.

As we continue to navigate the complex and ever-evolving frontier of free speech, it's worthwhile to reflect on policies such as the Fairness Doctrine. Although scrapped, its influence on our understanding of the responsibility of broadcasting outlets to serve public interest continues to hold relevance in our current digital era.

In the next section, we will trace modern manifestations of the tensions between free speech and fair representation, examined through the lens of the transformative impact of the digital age. As we dig further into the notion of free speech, remember the lessons learned from the Fairness Doctrine and its attempt to strike a delicate balance on the airwaves.

Digital Era: Social Media and the New Frontier

In our exploration of free speech, we can't overlook the seismic shifts brought by the digital era. It's reshaping the contours of interaction and communication as we know it. The rise of social media has created a new frontier where the principles and boundaries of free speech are constantly tested and re-defined.

From Facebook to Twitter to newer entrants like TikTok, social media platforms have provided an unprecedented platform for self-expression. They have enabled instant communication on a global scale, while also offering the opportunity for even the most marginalized voices to be heard. While this democratization of expression has brought about positive social changes, it has also stirred a cauldron of legal and ethical challenges regarding free speech.

The balance between free speech and harmful content is a dynamic, ever-shifting line in the sand, particularly in the digital discourse. Addressing this challenge involves scrutinizing a range of complex issues. These include the interpretation of the First Amendment within digital spaces, the user agreements on social media platforms, and the potential impact of erroneous or misleading information.

Unquestionably, the interpretation of the First Amendment has been stretched thin in the digital age. Online, you'll find a wide chasm between what's considered legally acceptable and what's deemed moral or ethical. This is particularly true when it comes to hate speech, which is technically protected under the Constitution, provided it doesn't incite violence.

However, it's important to remember that social media platforms, as private companies, can set their rules regarding permissible content. In other words, though the government can't limit speech based on its content or viewpoint, private entities can. This creates a complicated dynamic where constitutional principles of free speech intersect with corporate rights and responsibilities.

Adding to the complexity is the often murky user agreements on social media platforms. These agreements, which lay out what content is permitted, are constructed with a broad language to cover a multitude of scenarios. Often, users find themselves inadvertently crossing these lines, leading to content removal, account suspension, or even permanent bans.

On one hand, this can protect communities from harmful content. On the other, these agreement clauses and their enforcement can sometimes stifle free speech. But without these rules, we could run the risk of allowing hate speech, false information, or other harmful content to spread unchecked.

This brings us to the problem of misinformation. In the social media age, erroneous or misleading information can spread like wildfire, influencing public opinion and sometimes even

causing real-world harm. The dilemma lies in distinguishing between free speech and harmful misinformation.

This is an area where the term "fake news" often comes into play. Despite its misuse and misappropriation in recent years, fake news – false information deliberately spread to deceive or mislead – is a real issue in today's digital communication. It's a key concern when considering responsible free speech in our digital age.

Even though platforms such as Facebook and Twitter use algorithms and fact-checking tools to combat misinformation, fake news continues to prosper. This is due chiefly to the very nature of social media, which prioritizes engagement and shareability. In turn, sensational headlines and outrageous claims often get more attention, regardless of their accuracy.

The democratic ideal put forth by social media, wherein any individual can share their thoughts or opinions, lends itself well to the proliferation of misinformation. Misinformation, even when unintentionally spread, can have wide-reaching ramifications – from influencing political perceptions to harming public health.

On a grander scale, the proliferation of misinformation presents a significant challenge to the notion of free speech itself. When falsehoods are freely disseminated and believed, they undermine the fundamental purpose of free speech: to promote an informed, open society.

This makes it crucial to formulate a nuanced approach to managing the balance between freedom of speech and the challenges brought by social media. It is not a simple task, nor is it solely the responsibility of social media companies. Rather, it requires a collective effort by individuals, technology companies, lawmakers, and society as a whole.

Ultimately, although social media has complicated our understanding and application of free speech, it has also provided us with an opportunity to revisit our constitutional principles and adapt them to our digital landscape.

As the journey into the digital era continues to evolve, so too will our understanding of free speech. By applying and consistently re-evaluating our understanding of its principles within the context of social media, we can continually push to further our democratic ideals and safeguard the essence of free speech in America.

Chapter 3:
When Speech Becomes a Crime:
Understanding Illegal Expressions

In the great dance between freedom and law, it's crucial to understand the line that differentiates free speech from illegal expressions. The crux of the matter hinges on the notion of 'incitement to imminent lawless action.' Imagine, for a moment, you're passionately airing your grievances about particular injustices. Typically, this form of discourse isn't problematic, but if your rhetoric involves exhortations to imminent violence or causes panic that compromises public safety, you could be on thin ice. This is because the Supreme Court decided in Brandenburg v. Ohio that speech can be suppressed if it is likely to incite or produce such action. Moreover, 'fighting words'—speech intended to incite an immediate breach of the peace—land squarely in the realm of prohibited discourse. Likewise, 'true threats' ring some serious alarm bells in the legal landscape. These are speech or expressions that convey an immediate intent to commit an unlawful act of violence against an individual or group. Recall, the First Amendment exists to protect your voice, not your right to incite harm. In this chapter, we'll delve deeper into the labyrinth of legalities surrounding free speech, and examine how some seemingly innocuous words can shift from being protected expressions to unlawful actions, given the right—or rather wrong—context.

Incitement to Imminent Lawless Action

Shifting gears slightly, let's now focus on understanding the concept of 'incitement to imminent lawless action.' It's a phrase you might've heard in the news media, or perhaps during a law class, if you've brushed up against Constitutional Law. The Supreme Court, in Brandenburg v. Ohio, stared down this very issue, as we'll soon see.

The Brandenburg test, as it's known, is a two-pronged standard established by the Supreme Court in 1969. The Court ruled that governmental prohibitions on speech can't take effect unless the speech meets two specific thresholds. First, the speech must be intended to incite or produce imminent lawless action. Second, it must be likely that, as a consequence of the speech, this imminent lawless action will actually occur. Consistently applying this test discourages the censorship of provocative speech, while at the same time, prohibits expressions aimed solely to generate chaos and unlawful activities.

Let's take a moment here for clarification. The term 'imminent' doesn't mean sometime in the distant future, but something on an immediate horizon that is about to happen. Pondering this in the context of free speech elevates our understanding of the word. For instance, angry diatribes demanding that retribution be sought 'someday' or urging general, unspecified acts of rebellion don't cross the boundary of the Brandenburg test. However, speeches mentoring a crowd towards immediate violence likely will. Understand that this isn't a sign of free speech limitations, but rather, a necessity in balancing public safety with an individual's right to express their views. We'll explore other such parameters and balancing acts in the upcoming sections.

True Threats

As we navigate through the complexities of free speech, one imperative facet to examine is "true threats." The legal landscape takes a firm stance against true threats, those statements or actions that imply an intention to do harm. In essence, there's a line to be drawn between expressing an unpopular opinion and issuing a threat loaded with harmful intent. Though hotly debated, this critical distinction is crucial to preserving freedom while maintaining safety.

The concept of a 'true threat' emerged from a series of Supreme Court decisions, each case underscoring that freedom of speech doesn't provide a blanket cover for threats, intimidation, or incitement to violence. The rationale is clear: the individual's right to express their opinion should not endanger the life, liberty, or personal security of others. This understanding helps maintain a delicate balancing act between protecting free speech and preventing the potential harm that can stem from its abuse.

It's crucial to note that characterizing a statement as a 'true threat' isn't a simple process. The courts consider various factors, from how a reasonable person would interpret the statement to the circumstances surrounding its utterance. Additionally, context matters greatly in such designations and can tilt the balance dramatically in one direction or another. Consequently, understanding true threats involves unwrapping a complex layers of legal analysis and societal consequence, underscoring once again that free speech is not an absolute, but a privilege that requires rigorous, responsible stewardship.

Obscenity

The concept of obscenity is one that oscillates within the vast panorama of free speech. One may question, what constitutes obscenity in speech or expression and do such expressions have a place within the reaches of the First Amendment? The Supreme Court in America has wrestled with these questions and over the decades, they've landed on a somewhat malleable definition. In essence, an obscene act must, among other criteria, elicit 'prurient interest', depict sexual conduct in a 'patently offensive way', and lack serious 'value'— a rule famously known as the Miller test.

Despite the illusion of straightforwardness, interpretation of the Miller test can be tricky and one strains to avoid dangerous subjectivity. For example, the judgment of what's considered 'value' in a piece can differ vastly from one individual to another. One may deem a lascivious painting as vulgar and without merit, while another perceives it as an audacious exploration of human sexuality or a robust critique of societal norms. This unavoidable subjectivity has provoked endless discussions and debates.

In this epoch of rapidly evolving thought and socially charged media, the juxtaposition of obscenity and free speech may be viewed as more poignant than ever before. Controversies crop up regularly, whether it's explicit content on television or provocative art installations. While our society has become more permissive in recent years, the law's interpretation on obscenity can frequently lag behind, causing tension, and sparking crucial conversations. As we continue to explore the boundaries of free speech in the following sections, we'll delve further into how cultural shifts and societal trends impact this critical aspect of American jurisprudence.

Fighting Words: The Limit of Free Speech

Played out on the grand stage of American democracy, the battle for free speech is hardly ever black and white. Navigating through its grey areas can be complicated, particularly when it comes to understanding the concept of 'fighting words,' a crucial limitation to free speech. Often misconstrued or overlooked, the doctrine of 'fighting words' posits that certain expressions, intended to incite violence or cause immediate harm, fall outside the scope of protected speech.

Imagine yourself standing in a keenly anticipated protest march. The air is palpable with tension as diverse viewpoints grapple for dominance. The speech you're permitted to use here isn't unfettered – it's proportionate to the potential risk it carries. If your words are likely to provoke an average person to react violently, then they're transgressing into the territory of 'fighting words.' That's the clear distinction: free speech doesn't give us a free pass to stir up violence.

This doctrine, although controversial, highlights the fine line between exercising constitutional rights and maintaining public order. But remember, not any offensive or insulting speech can be deemed as 'fighting words.' The incitement to violence has to be immediate and likely, not merely hypothetical or potential. In the next section, we'll delve into the role of media in shaping perceptions of free speech, followed by a dissection of the double-edged sword known as political correctness. We have quite a journey ahead, exploring the complex maze that is the First Amendment.

Defamation (Libel and Slander)

As we traverse the terrain of rights and restrictions of free speech, the ominous landscape of defamation comes into view. Defamation, which includes libel and slander, is where the free speech boundary sharpens. But seriously, what does defamation mean? To put it plainly, defamation involves the communication of false statements that can tarnish an individual's reputation. It's critical to draw the distinction between expressing an adverse opinion and uttering an injurious falsehood.

Let's delve a smidgen deeper. Libel and slander are the two subtypes under the broad umbrella of defamation. In essence, Libel deals with defamatory remarks in a fixed medium, such as writing or images. Picture a scandalous tabloid article based on uncorroborated allegations or a damaging tweet founded on falsehoods. Slander, on the other hand, pertains to spoken defamatory statements. This could be a rumor maliciously spread at a community gathering or false claims aired on a radio show. Remember though, the dividing line here is not the medium used, but the permanence of the statement; printed or written words tend to have lasting ramifications, hence they fall under libel.

But here's the kicker: a purported defamatory statement, whether libelous or slanderous, must pass some tests before it's deemed so. First, the statement must be false. Second, it must be presented as a fact rather than an opinion. Third, it must lead to actual harm to one's reputation. Fourth, it must be publicly communicated. And lastly, according to U.S. law, in instances when public figures are involved, there must be proof of 'actual malice' – meaning the defamer was aware the statement was false or showed reckless disregard for the truth. Grasping these elements can help us better understand where boundaries are drawn limiting free speech in defamation cases. From this perspective, we can ascertain that free speech rights don't operate in a vacuum. Rather, they hover within a complex network of social, ethical, and legal responsibilities.

Fraud

Yet another boundary that springs forth in the realm of free speech finds its origins in the deceptive practice commonly known as fraud. This penurious encroachment feeds on the manipulation of truth and veiled deceit and clearly delineates a boundary on the freedoms that the First Amendment safeguarded. The reason is pragmatic, booby-trapped rhetoric can often cause incalculable harm by exploiting trust, stealing identities, draining bank accounts, and shattering lives.

The law navigates the choppy currents of free speech and fraud with an inherent tension. Its essence resonates with the shared understanding that while it's integral to defend the uninhibited, robust, and wide-open discourse, it's equally vital to safeguard citizens from egregious harm. Just as you can't yell 'fire' in a crowded theater to incite panic, neither can you use words to deliberately dupe someone for self-enrichment, without consequence. With this inherent check, the legal framework deftly draws a line in the shifting sands of speech and deceptive malpractice, a line that, if crossed, invokes legal sanctions reliably as the tide.

This boundary may seem unmistakably clear, but it offers its own challenges and paradoxes. For instance, how does the law distinguish an ingenious marketing tactic from a calculated scam? Where does enthusiastic exaggeration end and deceit begin? As we delve deeper into these questions, we'll examine the ripple effects that these scenarios create within the confines of free speech. Nonetheless, it stands to reason that while the freedom of speech is a hallowed constitutional right, the misuse of language for fraudulent ends is both a legal wrong and a social injury.

Extortion

Now, let's delve into another significant area that often interact with free speech: extortion. Defined generally, extortion refers to the act of unlawfully obtaining property, including money, or forcing actions from another person by threatening them. Of course, in the realm of communication and expression, this presents a prickly issue.

Imagine receiving a menacing message from an anonymous person, demanding that you do something specific or face embarrassing leaks about your personal life or loved ones. Alarming, isn't it? That's because our legal system is designed to protect citizens from such intimidation and victimization, drawing a clear, immovable line at coercion. The potential conflict with free speech arises when the act of extortion hinges upon the spoken or written word. While freedom of speech allows us to express our thoughts without fear of reprisal, it doesn't offer an umbrella of immunity for threats, coercion, or the use of fear to elicit compliance.

Thus, in the nexus of extortion and freedom of speech, the framework of the law becomes paramount. Acts of extortion are considered criminal behavior, irrespective of the method used to communicate the threat. Simply put, the right to free speech doesn't deliver a free pass to violate others' rights or commit crimes. Consequently, accurately defining the scope of free speech requires acknowledging the serious issue of extortion, and recognizing the necessary limits placed upon our freedom for the sake of ensuring personal safety and societal well-being.

Perjury

While we can find the term perjury in TV series and newspapers, a comprehensive understanding of this phenomenon is often not clear in our collective mind. Thus, let's delve deeper into this significant topic. Perjurers, committing a serious crime, are individuals who intentionally lie under oath during a deposition, court trial, or in a written statement. Their deliberate deception, vital to our judiciary system, doesn't represent an attack on free speech. It represents an assault on our collective trust, and our shared goal for truth-seeking in legal proceedings.

Before we dive into the relation between free speech and perjury, let's make clear that perjury is not protected by "free speech" grounds. It's a situation of deliberate fabrication or distortion of truth, posing direct harm to justice. Inevitably, truth finds itself at the intersection of both freedom and regulation. Our First Amendment doesn't grant us the freedom to misrepresent facts and manipulate the course of justice. It gives us the liberty to share our opinions and ideas, barring some exceptions, without government interference.

We shouldn't perceive perjury as a simple case of dishonesty, because its implications run deep. Perjury can shatter lives, warp our understanding of truth, and destabilize the foundations of our judicial processes. Indeed, this understanding can prove perverse for those who view free speech as an absolute. But we have to comprehend that rights don't exist in a vacuum. Other rights and values—like truth, justice, and trust—must interact harmoniously with our freedom of speech. Ultimately, as we continue to navigate the broader theme of free speech, it's essential to understand how these boundaries are absolutely essential to define the integrity of our free speech.

Solicitation of a Crime

In the uncharted terrain of free speech, the solicitation of a crime presents a particularly complex challenge. At its core, it refers to the act of inciting, encouraging, or persuading someone else to commit an illegal activity. For instance, offering a financial reward for committing a murder, though you're not the one physically pulling the trigger, it's your words fueling the action.

The First Amendment, while an admirable guard of our freedom of expression, doesn't provide an unconditional shield. In effect, it can't be used as a hiding place for promoting illegal activities or causing harm. Solicitation of a crime is closely scrutinized by our justice system, and individuals can be held accountable if their words can be demonstrably linked to illegal activities. Yet, it calls for careful maneuvering. We can't paradoxically punish free speech in the process of preserving it, a balance that's no easy task to strike.

Understanding the distinction drawn between advocacy and solicitation is crucial. Our courts have consistently protected the right to advocate for illegal activities in an abstract manner, understanding this as part of larger debates on contentious issues. You're free to argue the merits of tax evasion, for example, but actively persuading others to dodge their taxes is a different matter. Striking this balance ensures that our vital vein of free expression isn't severed, while also providing the necessary protection from damaging and harmful language. This way, the true spirit of free speech is upheld, while keeping a check on its misuse.

Blackmail

Blackmail, by its very nature, represents a dark underbelly of communication, a perversion of the concept of free speech. It uses the threat of releasing information to force specific behaviors or actions, tapping into an individual's fear for personal gain. Starkly contrary to the pursuit of free speech, blackmail abuses what's often sensitive or private information as a weapon. In essence, it's the antithesis of what free speech should encourage: the open, respectful exchange of ideas.

The reprehensible practice of blackmail is fundamentally oppressive and in stark contrast to the principles of transparency, accountability, and honesty that underline healthy communication. Blackmail crimps the space of open discussion by turning communication into a tool of manipulation. It's a tool that doesn't encourage dialogue or discussion–rather, it demands silence and compliance. Its very existence is contradictory to the core of free speech, a realm that ought to promote discourse, truth, and understanding.

When observing the landscape of free speech through the legal lens, the law confronts blackmail's stark contradiction to the principle of liberty. Any form of speech that thrives off manipulation and fear, rather than respect and openness, cannot remain excused under free speech protections. Having an understanding of free speech means recognizing that our communication must be free, yes, but also mustn't be corrosive to another's freedom. After all, when speech is turned into a weapon of manipulation, it doesn't just tarnish the nobility of our words— it diminishes the essence of our freedom.

Conspiracy

In the context of free speech, the issue of conspiracy theories emerges as an intriguing topic. Some might argue that the unfettered right to share and spread unfounded theories falls under protected speech. However, this perspective raises questions about the impact of harmful conspiracy theories on the democratic fabric of our society. It's important to understand, the freedom to express oneself doesn't necessarily include an unfettered license to spread false or harmful information that can erode the credibility of facts and generate societal discord.

Conspiracy theories can be a product of free speech pushed to its extreme, essentially a scenario where any claim is given equal weight, regardless of the evidence supporting it. It's a slippery slope, as it challenges our commitment to free speech when that very freedom appears to undermine our shared reality. An instance of such a dilemma can be seen in the dissemination of unsubstantiated claims during election periods, that are not only false but also potentially disastrous for the election process. Does the protection of free speech extend to these harmful fabrications, even when they risk tearing at the seams of our democracy?

As discerning citizens and advocates of free speech, the onus is on us to maintain a critical eye, interrogating the sources, motives, and credibility of the information we consume and share. The question isn't merely about curtailing free speech, rather it's about refining our collective understanding and usage of this right, to ensure we're contributing to a democratic society informed by truth, rather than falsehoods. Insisting on a commitment to truth in discourse doesn't weaken our commitment to free speech; instead, it strengthens it, as it protects from the fragility of misuse and its potential to inflict harm.

False Advertising

The discourse on false advertising segues perfectly from our discussion on incitement. Like an inciter promising mayhem and violence, the purveyor of false advertising lures us with dishonest claims. However, instead of inciting fear, a false advertiser incites belief in a fantasy, a dreamy version of reality that, unfortunately, doesn't exist.

False advertising typically finds itself in the caustic crosshairs of two cherished American values - capitalism and First Amendment freedoms. We often fail to realize, in our haste to decry every falsified claim or embellished boast, that not all untruths fall into the category of false advertising. It's not illegal, for instance, to exaggerate or boast. To qualify as false advertising, lies must not only distort the truth but also mislead a significant portion of the public, affect purchasing decisions, and induce individuals to pay for goods or services they wouldn't otherwise have wanted.

So, while we navigate the blurred lines of truth and falsehood in advertising, let's remember that the law often permits puffery and certain types of exaggeration. Such allowances don't serve to protect advertisers but to protect the principle of free speech and our collective right to decide for ourselves what to purchase and from whom. Of course, malicious lies meant to defraud or harm should and will be penalized. But it's not the lie that's the problem; it's the intent. And this very nuance plays a crucial role in defining the parameters of false advertising in our society.

Harassment

In our quest to define and understand the complex nature of free speech, we've come across a crucial boundary – harassment, an area where the parameters of freedom collide with the obligation to respect individual rights. In a democratic society, free speech is essential for open discourse and progress. However, when political ideologies transmogrify into an invitation to attack, belittle, or intimidate, it becomes necessary to distinguish between the constitutional right to express oneself and destructive aggression.

This in no way suggests we're advocating for a throttling down of free dialogue, it's merely a proposition of exercising rights without intruding on another's peace of mind. An integral part of living in a society is understanding that the right to swing your fist ends where another's nose begins. Similarly, vocal advocacy for your viewpoint doesn't necessarily have to involve a disparaging act aimed at demeaning others. Retaining the ethos of free speech requires a delicate act of balance, straddling the fine line between tolerance for diverse opinions and granting a license for targeted harassment.

Harassment manifests in multifarious ways, from persistent annoyance to outright threats, or repeated, unwanted attention with intent to upset or harm. And herein lies the rub: how can we precisely define when free speech becomes harassment, a watershed that's often blurred and subjective? Context, intent, and impact are key elements in this determination. It's far from an easy task, but as we move forward with the discussion on setting up boundaries for free speech, it's certainly a challenge we're committed to addressing.

Trade Secrets

The vast arena of speech extends beyond personal interactions and public discourse, and notably stretches into the sphere of business and trade. While as a society we champion principles of transparency and information sharing, we simultaneously acknowledge the necessity of certain protections – including trade secrets. These are vital to maintaining competitive edges, fostering innovation, and fortifying economic vigor.

Trade secrets, by definition, are information that companies keep confidential to gain a business advantage. This may include production methods, customer lists, software algorithms, recipes, or operational strategies. Under US law, protected by the Economic Espionage Act of 1996, revealing such information without consent is a federal crime. It's an interesting caveat to the broad interpretation and application of free speech, reminding us that the right is not, and perhaps can't be, absolute. Privacy rights, business interests, and economic stability are just as powerful and necessary within our system—a testament to the convoluted nature of navigating rights and defining boundaries.

Yet, even within the context of trade secrets, exceptions surface. Creative, yet lawful techniques, commonly referred to as competitive intelligence, allow companies to gather information about their rivals. Think traditional market research, product comparisons, or hiring industry consultants for advice. Amidst the interplay of transparency and secrecy, competition and protection, free speech remains a complex collage of layered rights. As we delve further into this book, analyzing different forms of information control, ranging from censorship to informational security, we hope to spotlight the nuances of free speech and its intertwining with other equally cherished rights and principles we hold as a society.

Disclosure of Classified Information

Peeling back the heavy curtains of secrecy and unveiling the hidden truths, that's the job, the arduous task, of those intrepid enough to devote themselves to investigative journalism. Yet, when one stumbles upon classified information, the looming question is whether speaking out crosses the line or is justified under the broad canopy of free speech. The complex dance between public interest and national security is, without any doubt, a contentious issue within the boundaries of free speech.

It's critical to focus on the facts. The First Amendment does not grant an absolute right to divulge, willy-nilly, classified information, especially when that disclosure threatens our national security. Laws such as the Espionage Act of 1917, in place for more than a century now, plainly lay out the criminal penalties for individuals handling sensitive information irresponsibly. There are good reasons behind this, like maintaining diplomatic relations and ensuring the safety of the nation's citizens. Yet it's not always as clear cut as it seems - one person's safeguard can be seen as another's muzzle.

Enter whistleblowers, the men and women behind the scenes who raise the alarm when they perceive ill-doings, corruption, or threats to public health or safety. Their role has been invaluable in shedding light on hidden truths, but the nature of their disclosures can sometimes render them on the wrong side of the law. A case in point was the Pentagon Papers scandal, which redefined the scope of First Amendment rights and pressed into question the government's ability to suppress the media in the name of national security. Must one man's liberty to inform the public be chained to prohibitive legal statutes? Or, in certain circumstances, can the disclosure of classified information contribute to the public good? These are questions which continue to define the discourse of free speech in America today.

Copyright Infringement

Delving into the sphere of Copyright Infringement, it's essential to grasp how this factor plays itself out in the realm of free speech. Just as freedom possesses its boundaries, so too does copyright, and it's important to respect those limits. Copyright law safeguards the original work of creators from being exploited without consent or due reward, acting as a boundary to protect ingenious inventiveness. Copyright infringement, then, is the encroachment or trespassing of that boundary, and it's an act that can swiftly pull free speech into a legal quagmire.

Steering your way around the murky waters of copyright infringement often requires a nuanced understanding of fair use and parodies, which often stride a fine line between permissible homage and unlawful replication. Freedom of speech doesn't provide a carte blanche to use someone else's creative work without necessary permissions or licenses. There are, of course, exceptions - under certain circumstances, copyrighted material can be used without the owner's permission. These typically fall under 'fair use', which allows the utilization of copyrighted works for criticism, news reporting, teaching, scholarship, and research, among other things.

Infringing on someone's copyright is a serious offense that can lead to hefty penalties and legal fees. The balance between preserving individual free speech rights and protecting the creative contributions of artists, writers, and others is a delicate dance, one the judicial system finds itself constantly navigating. Therefore, understanding the boundaries of speech as they apply to copyright infringement is a fundamental part of a broader comprehension of what free speech really means in our society.

Doxing

The rising interest in social justice has triggered a new, disturbing phenomenon: Doxing. This practice involves the unauthorized release of private information--names, addresses, and other identifying data--on the internet. Free speech proponents argue that this activity is a form of expression, a way for the powerless to hold the powerful to account. Detractors, however, see it as a gross violation of privacy. These conflicting views underscore the complexities of free speech in our digital age.

Imagine a scenario where someone posts misleading or false information leading to undeserved backlash. Targeted individuals, subject to doxing, might find their lives irrevocably damaged. There are stories of people losing their jobs, having their reputations tarnished, or even fearing for their lives. Despite this, some argue if you've chosen to engage in public discourse, you've tacitly agreed to be held accountable for your words, suggesting that the threat of doxing acts as a deterrent to harmful speech or behavior.

The legal angle isn't straightforward. Strictly speaking, if the information released is publicly available and not used for illegal purposes, like harassment, then it may not be punishable. But the line often blurs. Furthermore, the advent of the internet has made personal data more accessible, increasing the potential for misuse. Legal experts and law enforcement agencies grapple with these nuances as they work to strike a balance between freedom of expression and protecting individuals from undue harm. When it comes to doxing, it seems the line between free speech and privacy invasion is murky, and requires careful navigation.

Hate Speech

In our quest to uphold the principles of free speech, we find ourselves at an intriguing crossroads when it's time to discuss hate speech. Characterized by communication that demeans or devalues others on the basis of their ethnicity, race, religion, gender, or other protected characteristics, hate speech has become a societal menace. It's something that seems to polarize the very fabric of our understanding of what it means to express oneself freely.

Unrestrained words that breed hatred and mistrust tear at the heart of a free society, jeopardizing the ideal of 'liberty and justice for all'. However, imposing restrictions on speech is undeniably a slippery slope, teetering on the brink of possibly curtailing legitimate modes of expression. On one hand, we can't disregard the potential of hate speech in inciting violence or fostering discrimination. On the other, we don't want to infringe upon the rights of individuals to articulate personal opinions and beliefs. Striking the ideal balance seems akin to walking a constitutional tightrope.

As the law currently stands in the United States, the freedom of speech is not an absolute right. The assessment of what constitutes hate speech often derives from the litmus test of whether it incites 'imminent lawless action'. This standard, established by the Supreme Court in the landmark case of Brandenburg v. Ohio (1969) has been the cornerstone of adjudications concerning hate speech, tolerating inflammatory speech unless it is likely to lead to immediate harm. However, the complexities involved in qualifying and quantifying this 'immediacy' of harm frequently raise sharp debates. In the forthcoming chapters, we will delve deeper into the machinations of this particular aspect of free speech law and its implications on our society.

Cyberbullying

Freedom of speech is a constitutional grandeur that has stood the test of time, guarding the audacious vivacity of our democracy. However, when this prerogative plunges into the wilderness of the Internet, it captivates an unsettling doppelgänger best identified as cyberbullying. On the surface, it seems slightly eccentric to try and tangle up cyberbullying with free speech. One boasts of liberty and progression, and the other is a vile and venomous weapon. But here's the conundrum: the very foundation of free speech can turn into a cloak for those orchestrating a destructive crescendo of cyber abuse.

Cyberbullying could be referred to as the alter ego of free speech in the digital scape, empowered and emboldened by anonymity. Online platforms act as amplifiers, carrying the echoes of taunts, threats, and torments into every corner of cyberspace. Stories of devastation from the victims of cyberbullying are both heartbreaking and alarming. Those bearing the brunt of such attacks often find themselves in a paradoxical state: on one hand, they feel the ruthless sting of these public attacks, yet paradoxically, total isolation. A key issue is determining when free speech ends and harassment begins, requiring a careful balancing of rights and protections.

The challenge lies in teasing apart these tangled threads, to reintroduce free speech in its pure, unadulterated form, free from the devastating stench of cyberbullying, without curtailing the expressional freedom. We must remember, the goal of free speech was never to arm the oppressors, but to amplify the voices that quietly resist oppression. We can't afford to remain muted spectators in this high-stakes battle. We need to be able to facilitate the harmony of differing perspectives, while simultaneously stamping out this strain of abuse that threatens to taint the spirit of free speech. The palpable paradox of free speech resides in its ability to be both a shield and a sword. The balancing act here is as critical as it is precarious, and it is one that we can't afford to get wrong.

False Reports

Skirting the edge of the First Amendment, we find a gray area, misleadingly adorned with the title of 'False Reports'. A potentially dangerous realm of free speech, false reports demonstrate the need for our legal norms to change and adapt in the face of social and technological evolution.

False reports—or "fake news," as they're more commonly known—can threaten public safety and undermine democracy if left unchecked; they were not what our Founding Fathers intended to foster under the shield of the First Amendment. The protection of free speech, central to American society, does not serve as an enabling force for malice. Instead, it seeks to cultivate an environment that encourages reasoned discourse, accurate reporting, and the free exchange of truthful information. It's crucial to understand, however, that this does not give one the right to spread false information that can harm others or incite violence.

Current laws that grapple with this issue - such as defamation or libel laws - were woven into the fabric of our legal system as remedies against false reports, but they often fall short in the digital age. Digital platforms have transformed the way information is shared, making it challenging to trace, regulate, and hold accountable false report origins. It is essential to rethink our current legal structures and establish stronger legal definitions to manage false reports in the age of the digital revolution effectively. From the lenses of a legal expert, the battle against false reports is not only about establishing legal boundaries but also about reinforcing ethical ones in promoting truthful speech.

Contempt of Court

Freedom of speech isn't absolute. Contempt of Court serves as a tangible example of how speech can test constitutional boundaries. This term generally denotes a behavior that disrespects the court's authority, but it notably includes any mode of speech that may disrupt court proceedings or impede justice. Speaking out unfairly against a judge, questioning the credibility of the court, or knowingly disregarding court rules are actions that can earn you a citation for contempt of court. Moreover, if those words reach the broader public, there's potential for a wildfire of misinformation, which can effectively taint a jury pool or otherwise obstruct facets of the judicial process.

There's inherent value in guarding against false narratives and preserving the integrity of our court system. Acknowledging this, the First Amendment doesn't grant a free pass to flagrantly manipulate or disrespect the judiciary through harmful language. Even under the protection of free speech, there's a point where the scale tips, and our words morph into actions that risk crippling the justice system. This delicate balance illustrates the law's innate effort to strike a fair compromise between an individual's right to expression and upholding the societal interest in preserving a fair and functional judiciary.

However, identifying this tipping point isn't always clear-cut, and navigating contempt of court can be like treading a harrowing tightrope. Its implications aren't limited to the courtroom. How much should we tolerate strident criticism of our justice system, particularly in the public arena, before it becomes contemptuous? In this context, freedom of speech enters a tense standoff with judicial authority and must often be carefully reeled in to prevent the corrosion of faith in our legal institutions. Moving forward, we'll delve into further specifics, exploring how this crucial interplay between freedom of speech and our judiciary continues to shape our understanding of free expression in America.

Restraining Orders/Protective Orders

At this juncture, it's crucial to acknowledge how protective orders, often termed restraining orders, contribute to our perceptions of free speech. These orders can, and often do, place specific limitations on someone's ability to communicate freely, but for substantiated, often safety-related reasons. While they may seem on the surface to oppose the First Amendment's tenets, their application actually embodies the idea of free speech–it's not about unlimited expression, but finding balance in respecting the rights and safety of every individual.

You're probably wondering how a law that explicitly limits communication can align with the notion of free speech. It helps to remember that free speech, as a concept, doesn't advocate for a person to harm, harass, or infringe upon another's rights. Instead, the intent is to enable a platform for expressing opinions, discussing ideas, and promoting dialogue without government interference. This is where protective orders come into play; they serve to protect individuals from harassment, violence, or other forms of harm, ensuring that one's free speech does not impinge on the rights and safety of another.

The acknowledgment of protective orders reminds us that free speech is not an excuse to foster malicious communication. It nudges us to practice responsible expression and respect the boundaries of others' rights. A broad perspective reveals that these orders align with the larger objective of free speech - promoting an environment of respect, dialogue, and diversity. In other words, these orders are not opposing or repressing free speech, instead they regulate it to maintain safety, respect, and harmony within the society whilst preserving the essence of the First Amendment's principles.

Commercial Speech

Any discourse breezing through your mind at this moment likely ascribes 'speech' to the domain of interpersonal communication or public debate. Nonetheless, free speech extends much farther and engulfs even the realm of commerce. Commercial Speech, as it is aptly named, encompasses all expressions made by businesses intended to persuade consumers and expedite transactions. This facet of free speech flies unobtrusively under the radar of regulations and public scrutiny, yet stirs profound ripple effects through the breadth and depth of our economic, social and personal spaces.

Commercial Speech is no stranger to legal controversy. Understanding its crux, one must traverse back to the 1970s landmark Supreme Court case of Virginia State Board of Pharmacy v. Virginia Citizens Consumer Council. Herein lays a firm lineament in the sands of legal precedence, where for the first time, commercial speech was provided protection under the First Amendment. The acknowledgment of the consumers' interest in receiving information was of primordial importance, transforming advertising into an arena of 'speech'. Consequently, this ruling rang the death knell for the era wherein commercial entities were stymied from employing the trappings of First Amendment.

Deftly navigating the labyrinthine nature of Commercial Speech and the Free Speech protections it hollers for demands scrutiny. On one hand, limitations are sometimes necessary to prevent manipulative and deceptive practices, safeguarding the consumer populace. Conversely, fettering the free reign of businesses to communicate can undermine the open market's dynamism, throttling economic growth. Mitigating these competing tensions necessitates not only a masterful understanding of the law, but also the functions and implications of commercial speech. Indeed, the implications of how boundaries define free speech within the commercial world are manifold and far-reaching.

Regulated Industries

When examining the issue of free speech, it is crucial that we consider the concept within the context of regulated industries. Certain sectors of the U.S. economy face stringent regulations, sometimes even impacting the speech of organizations and individuals involved in them. But don't be mistaken; this isn't always as ominous as it may sound. These regulations serve to protect consumers, market integrity and maintain fair competition.

In the world of finance, for instance, there are explicit regulations regarding what information can be shared about a company's financial health or future prospects. These regulations aim to prevent situations where insiders might use their privileged access to sensitive financial information for personal gain, at the risk of damaging the economic system. Similarly, in the pharmaceutical industry, companies are heavily regulated in terms of what they can say in their advertisements. The goal here is to ensure public health safety, by preventing companies from making unproven or misleading health claims about their products. In this way, free speech rights are sometimes tempered by urgent public interest concerns.

The crux of the matter is finding a balance between free speech and these regulating rules. It's essential to understand that First Amendment rights do not equate to an absolute freedom to share any information at any time. Constraints are often necessary to uphold the rule of law, maintain order, and ensure societal well-being. Yet, it's a delicate dance between preserving our hard-earned liberties and protecting the common good. With this as our backdrop, we'll move on to explore other areas that test the boundaries of free speech in the next chapters.

Chapter 4:
Navigating Murky Waters: Morally Problematic Speech

As we delve into the dubious realm of morally problematic speech, we find ourselves walking a labyrinthine judicial tightrope. This area of free speech, although protected under the First Amendment, prompts a host of intricate questions about ethics, legal boundaries, and societal norms. After all, is inflammatory hate speech—laden with racist, sexist, or homophobic slurs—considered legitimate self-expression? Or should it be viewed as a violation of public safety akin to shouting "fire" in a crowded theater? There's no simple answer. One valuable perspective, however, is that free speech isn't an absolute right, but rather a public good that needs to be balanced with other societal interests. Content that intentionally incites violence or direct harm towards individuals or specific groups is typically not tolerated under U.S law. Yet, provocative speech that simply offends or challenges the status quo can indeed fall within legal parameters. It's a tricky equilibrium, maintaining a vital balance between safeguarding our democratic liberties and protecting the dignity and safety of every citizen. The next chapters will continue to dissect this balance, exploring the legal delineations of offensive speech, the intersection of free speech and social media, and the broader impacts of these discussions on our society as a whole.

The Rise of Disinformation and Fake News

The world has witnessed an alarming surge in disinformation and fake news, with America being no exception. This newfound prevalence dances with the concept of free speech. While the foundation of democracy offers a platform for freedom of expression, the twisted propagation of fabrications gets lost in the fray.

Critics of free speech often argue that it's an enabling mechanism for disinformation. Nevertheless, it's essential to understand that it's not the notion of free speech in itself that fosters this chaos, but the abuse and manipulation of it that do.

The phenomenon of 'fake news,' while not a novel concept, has undeniably gained prominence in the era of digital media and diversified information dissemination channels. From social networks to message-sharing chat forums, these platforms serve as a breeding ground for disinformation, leading to a crisis of truth.

The mechanic is simple: a piece of misleading or false information gets created, it's shared multiple times across platforms, and the frequency of its sharing validates it in the minds of consumers. This phenomenon has been amplified due to the speedy spread of information on social media.

This sinister dance of disinformation has grave repercussions, ranging from individual misunderstandings to societal upheaval. Conspiracy theories, wrongful allegations, and crafted narratives have led to violent events, wrongful persecution, and a general state of distrust at a collective level. This is a frightening deviousness enabled by the distortion of free speech's pure concept.

The dilemma becomes about discerning the fine line between free speech and the spread of harmful falsehoods. One man's right to express an opinion can morph into a society's nightmare, especially when that opinion is based on misinformation and repeated until it's perceived as truth.

The law, however, isn't devoid of mechanisms to deal with disinformation. Courts in the United States have consistently maintained that false statements of fact lack constitutional value. Yet, distinguishing between genuine errors and deliberate falsehoods proves challenging, not to mention the difficulty of adjudicating truth in a contentious, polarized climate.

An important aspect of this discussion is the responsibility of digital platforms in controlling disinformation. These platforms, including Internet Service Providers (ISPs), are protected under Section 230 of the Communications Decency Act, which states that they can't be treated as publishers of the information shared on their platforms by third-party users.

Yet, critics argue that this protection has granted these platforms a "get out of jail free card." The argument is particularly potent given the pervasive nature of these platforms in the dissemination of not just neutral information, but vitally, disinformation.

Another challenge lies in the enforcement of laws against disinformation. Victimization due to misinformation is rarely discrete, with effects diffused across a population. This often makes legal recourse challenging, if not downright impossible.

Yet hope is not lost. Much work is being done across industries to tackle this issue. Fact-checking organizations have proliferated, working tirelessly to debunk false narratives. Various tools and initiatives are being developed to support the verification of information.

Beyond this, discussions on a legal and policy level are underway to understand how to hold those who maliciously spread falsehoods accountable, without infringing upon the sacred tenets of free speech.

This battle against disinformation, it seems, will be a defining feature of our time. The shaping of this narrative, and the molding of the policies that govern it, will fundamentally redefine our understanding of free speech in the digital age.

In essence, the rise of disinformation and fake news is not a condemnation of free speech, but rather a manifestation of its perversion. It serves as a stark reminder of the double-edged sword that free speech can be, if improperly wielded or interpreted.

While the road towards understanding and resolving this issue may seem long and winding, it's a journey that society will inevitably embark upon, marking yet another significant juncture in the ongoing evolution of free speech and its boundaries.

Controversial Art and the Freedom of Expression

Freedom of expression is a robust cornerstone of the American Constitution. It's a fundamental right treasured and fiercely guarded by citizens. However, it's never as simple as it appears, especially when it entails controversial zones such as art.

Art— whether in the form of paintings, sculptures, performances, or films— has been a platform for individuals to express their perspectives. Yet, the boundary between freedom of expression and what's perceived as inappropriate, offensive, or blasphemous can often blur, giving rise to contentious debates and legal battles.

Consider Andres Serrano's infamous photograph, "Piss Christ". The artwork features a crucifix submerged in the artist's urine and has been described as both a profound statement on the commercialization and trivialization of religious icons in contemporary culture and as sacrilegious. While Serrano insisted on his right to freedom of expression, many religious groups were deeply offended by the artwork. Drawing a line between offense and freedom can be complex and subjective.

An artist's right to free speech in the United States is protected under the First Amendment unless it crosses into the territory of obscenity. But as Justice Potter Stewart famously quote in his judgment, "I know it when I see it," the line between art and obscenity can be remarkably unclear.

Robert Mapplethorpe's provocative photographs— vivid depictions of the LGBTQ+ community, BDSM, and nudity— have elicited mixed reactions and heated debate. Supporters laud the unflinching portrayal of marginalized communities and unconventional sexual practices, while critics decry it as pornographic, offensive, and against public morality.

So, does the presumed intent of the creator excuse the offense taken by the observer? There's no straightforward answer. Just as the freedom of expression protects the artist, it equally protects the audience's right to criticize, boycott, or protest art they perceive as offensive or inappropriate. Balancing both these rights presents a dilemma.

Furthermore, taxpayer funding of controversial art can further complicate matters. Should the public's tax dollars be used to fund art that much of the populace may find offensive? It's a question debated time and again with cases such as the National Endowment for the Arts (NEA) funding for controversial art, asking to what extent government institutions should support potentially offensive art in the name of freedom of expression.

In the case of the 1996 "NEA Four", the Supreme Court ruled that while the NEA has the right to consider "general standards of decency and respect" when awarding grants, imposing restrictions on content raises serious First Amendment questions. Thus, the balance between artistic freedom, public sentiment, and governmental support continues to be negotiated.

Artistic representation can often challenge status quo and confront deep-seated societal norms. It can provoke, inspire or aggravate. Whether it's Chris Ofili's "The Holy Virgin Mary" or the infamous Muhammad cartoons, art that critiques religious beliefs or institutions can ignite passions and protests.

Such incidents have sparked discussions on the boundaries of artistic freedom, raising questions about cultural sensitivity, the right to blasphemy, and religious expression. Despite grave consequences in some instances, these controversial artworks force us to redefine the meaning and limits of free speech.

The aspects discussed above illustrate the complicated relationship between art and free speech. They highlight that each piece of controversial art doesn't just challenge societal norms and perspectives, but also tests the perimeters of free speech itself. And it's up to legal experts, scholars, artists, and the public alike to navigate this complex landscape.

One must keep in mind, however, that the freedom of expression is not an absolute right. It always comes with limitations. But the challenge lies in preventing these limitations from becoming tools for stifling dissent and controlling narratives that challenge power structures. As we strive to understand and protect our right to free speech, we must ensure it doesn't become a casualty of blurred boundaries.

So, in this ongoing and ever evolving dialogue about freedom of expression, controversial art plays a crucial role in pushing boundaries and encouraging conversations. And although some may take offense, it's vital to remember that it's this very ability to offend and be offended, to provoke and be provoked, that forms the spirit of a truly free society.

After all, as they say, 'art is supposed to comfort the disturbed and to disturb the comfortable'. And perhaps, in the process, it brings us closer to the truest meaning and potential of free speech.

Blurred Lines: Satire, Parody, and Offensiveness

The fine line between satire and offensiveness is a subject of considerable deliberation in the realm of free speech. It is an age-old rhetorical device, both clever and contentious, that has created tension within societies. Satire, when done skillfully, is a powerful tool that can illuminate, critique, and challenge prevailing social, political, or moral norms. The concern emerges when a satirical representation crosses the boundary into the realm of offensiveness, and sparks divergent viewpoints regarding the limitations of our First Amendment rights.

Central to this discourse is the question: where does one draw the line? This challenge ties back to the basic principle of free speech – speech should not be suppressed unless it directly leads to harm. However, the interpretation of 'harm' is subjective, particularly when addressing the emotional or psychological distress someone may feel as a result of offensive satire.

An often-cited First Amendment principle is that the government cannot proscribe speech simply because it is offensive to some people. This tenet has been reaffirmed in several judicial decisions like the 1971 case of Cohen v. California where the U.S. Supreme Court ruled that the government could not criminally penalize a person for wearing a jacket bearing an offensive slogan in a courthouse. Yet, the unbridled utilization of this principle can blur the lines between freedom of speech and offensive speech, causing societal rifts.

Frequently forming part of this discourse is the concept of parody. A parody, akin to satire, uses humor, ridicule, or irony to criticize or ridicule its subject, usually for a comedic effect. However, like satire, parodies can inadvertently cause offense, particularly when the object of the parody feels misrepresented or unfairly targeted.

Parodies are generally protected under the First Amendment and have been recognized as such in numerous judgements. The landmark case of Campbell v. Acuff-Rose Music, Inc. (1994) established that a commercial parody can qualify as fair use, and be protected under the First Amendment. Yet, it's important to note a critical aspect – such legal protection doesn't necessarily guard the parody creators from public backlash or societal rebuke.

The considerations around satire and parody are further complicated by the anonymous and instant nature of the internet. Something meant as satire or parody can be taken out of context and spread rapidly, leading to unintended offense to a wider audience. The line between harmless jest and hurtful mockery can become increasingly thin within this digital realm.

Moreover, the ever-growing diversity of the American social fabric underscores the fine line separating satire or parody from offensiveness. Societal norms and perceptions of what is deemed 'acceptable' or 'offensive' are constantly evolving, driven by our expanding understanding of different cultures, races, religions, and identities.

This growing consciousness should not be misconstrued as a challenge to free speech, but rather, an evolution of social acceptability. It would be prudent to realize that the humor or critique ingrained in satire and parody can be interpreted differently based on the receiver's background, experience, perspective, and sensibilities. Hence, what may seem like a harmless jest to someone might constitute an offensive remark to someone else.

Nonetheless, the protection against 'hate speech' is a crucial deterrent to those who might misuse satire and parody under the guise of freedom of speech. While our First Amendment ensures a largely unrestricted platform for satire and parody, it does not shield expressions classifying as 'hate speech' that incites violence or promotes hostility against a particular group based on race, religion, gender, or similar attributes.

The discourse on satire, parody, and offensiveness in the context of free speech is unlikely to reach an all-encompassing consensus, considering the inherent subjective and diverse nature of these terms. Still, it's a dialogue that ought to continue, fostering a sophisticated understanding of the role and limitations of satire, parody, and offensiveness in our society.

Universally defining the permissible boundaries of satire, parody, and offense in free speech can seem a mammoth task, primarily due to the subjective variability among individuals and cultures. However, upholding the principles of empathy, respect, and decency might provide a foundation for individual judgement, creating a more inclusive discourse.

Finally, it's crucial to remember the underlying principle of the First Amendment – to maintain an environment conducive to "the uninhibited, robust, and wide-open" exchange of ideas. Constructive forms of satire and parody that challenge societal norms, stimulate critical thought, and encourage dialogues should therefore be championed. At the same time, we must equally ensure they do not become tools of cruelty, discrimination, or harm.

In conclusion, as our society advances, these blurred lines between satire, parody, and offensiveness will continue to shift. As with most aspects of our evolving constitutional jurisprudence, we will have to navigate the changing contours of this discourse, remaining mindful of the delicate balance between the freedom of speech and the potential for harm.

Culturally Sensitive Speech: Walking on Eggshells?

The idea of culturally sensitive speech may bring to mind an image of walking carefully, like one might walk on eggshells, to avoid offending individuals from different backgrounds. And indeed, the balancing act presents a set of challenges that one must grapple with when navigating the nuances of free speech in a diverse culture, but it isn't always as restrained or restricted as one might believe.

Traditionally, our concept of free speech has largely rested on John Stuart Mill's 'harm principle': the idea that one's liberty to act, (in this case, to speak), stops where it causes harm to another. This is obviously a simplification and one which has been called into question by various developments, but it is instructive in helping us understand what we consider 'harm' in relation to speech.

To delve into the sensitivity of culturally-focused speech, we must first look at the concept of 'cultural harm' and its implications on our understanding of free speech. Cultural harm could range from offhanded stereotypical representations to harmful caricatures, from denial or mockery of historical suffering to blatant racism. It, however, becomes harder to define clear boundaries of this harm and that's mainly why the nature of culturally sensitive speech can often be both vague and contentious.

One aspect that poses a significant challenge is the diverse nature of American society. With its rich mix of cultures, customs, languages, and traditions, understanding what might constitute offensive or harmful speech can be a complex task. Part of the difficulty arises from the fact that individuals and communities vary greatly in their views and resilience towards potentially offensive or disrespectful speech.

A phrase that might be offensive to one individual could be harmless to another. A cultural reference that one group sees as a tribute, another might view as mockery or cultural appropriation. This variance makes it nearly impossible to institute a universal set of guidelines or rules governing culturally sensitive speech.

Factors to Consider.
Several factors come into play when we consider culturally sensitive speech and its intersection with free speech. These include historical context, power dynamics, the impact of derogatory words or phrases, shared public values, and evolving societal norms.

Historical context is crucial in understanding culturally sensitive speech. Some words or phrases are offensive due to their historical use as derogatory terms. While these expressions may seem harmless in the present, their historical implications can still result in hurt and offense.

Power dynamics also play a role. Offensive speech can reinforce societal inequality, and so it is crucial to understand the power structures within a society. A joke by a member of a dominant group at the expense of a marginalized group can have different implications as compared to the same joke made within the marginalized group itself.

The direct, tangible impact of derogatory words or phrases is another factor to seriously consider. It's not just about feelings getting hurt. Derogatory speech can perpetuate stereotypes, reinforce discriminatory practices and even lead to violence.

Culturally Sensitive Speech in Practice.
In practice, aiming for culturally sensitive speech does not necessarily limit freedom of expression. Instead, it promotes a culture of empathy, respect, and consideration. It encourages us to be aware of diverse cultural experiences and understandings and to tailor our words accordingly.

Still, it's essential to recognize that legal measures alone can't fully address the issue of culturally sensitive speech. Instead, promoting a culture that upholds respect for others, values diversity, and encourages open dialogue can contribute significantly to addressing this issue.

Inevitably, there will always be debates and disagreements about what constitutes culturally sensitive speech. These conversations can themselves serve a vital role in fostering understanding and respect for differing cultural perspectives.

What's clear, however, is that culturally sensitive speech is not about walking on eggshells. It's about demonstrating respect and understanding for others' experiences and identities. It's not about stifling expression, but fostering a more inclusive discourse. Walking this path requires balance and understanding, but the end results - a society with greater respect for diversity and an overall richer discourse - make it all very worthwhile.

Chapter 5:
Drawing the Line:
The Ethics of Speech Boundaries

Now that we've waded into the morally murky waters of free speech, let's assess where and how we should draw the line. Effectively navigating the terrain of free speech rights demands more than a solid grasp of legal principles; it necessitates a deep dive into the philosophy behind the very concept. Free speech, at its core, is a question of balance—simultaneously tolerating diverse viewpoints while limiting harmful, unjust, or misleading communication. It's essential to acknowledge that while the First Amendment shields us from governmental censorship, it doesn't net the larger field of private entities. The complex interplay between governments, corporations, and individuals invites compelling ethical dilemmas: Who gets to control the narrative? How do we arbitrate between protection and access? Furthermore, it's not just about understanding our domestic reality. A global lens reveals a vast array of approaches to free speech regulations, casting our own situation into stark relief. Over the subsequent pages, we'll sift through the philosophical strata of free speech rights, probe the tension between tolerance and limitation, delve into the tricky terrain of private sector censorship, and look overseas in our quest to understand America's unique First Amendment legacy.

The Philosophical Underpinnings of Free Speech

Free speech is often praised as a cornerstone of democracy, a foundational principle upon which our nation was built. To truly understand the power and importance of free speech, it's crucial to delve into its philosophical underpinnings. Seeing beyond the legal landscape and toward the profound, philosophical implications, we expose the true significance.

At its essence, free speech carries an intrinsic link to individual autonomy. It fosters not just our ability but also our responsibility to express personal views, to critique, and to challenge. It's through this lens that philosopher John Stuart Mill regarded free speech as essential in the pursuit of truth. For Mill, all ideas, however controversial, should be open for discussion since only rigorous, public debate can sift fact from falsehood.

Mill's perspective, known as the 'marketplace of ideas' theory, suggests that in an open, competitive 'marketplace', truthful ideas ultimately rise to the top. Thus, we protect free speech - even speech we disagree with, or find offensive - because banning it assumes we are infallible in our judgment of what's right and wrong, true and false.

It's not just about truth, though. Free speech brings the important ability to express personal identity. It allows people to articulate ideas and beliefs integral to their individuality. In its absence, forced silence creates a sense of invisibility, pushing potentially impactful thoughts and innovators to the societal periphery.

A counterpoint to this though, is philosopher Ronald Dworkin's 'rights-based' approach, which proposes that all ideas should be heard on the principle of moral equality. He asserts that restricting speech undermines an individual's right to respect and equal consideration in society. Thus, free speech is less about the potential for truth-telling and more about our ethical obligation to fellow citizens.

Nevertheless, free speech isn't without philosophical critique. For some thinkers, free speech offers a faulty premise, giving all speakers a pretense of equal footing, while in reality, social, economic, and political forces often amplify some voices and mute others.

German philosopher Jürgen Habermas suggests a concept of 'discourse ethics', advocating communicative action based on mutual understanding and societal consensus. This recognizes that the ideal free speech landscape, in which all voices hold equal weight, is yet elusive.

In the context of power dynamics, French philosopher Michel Foucault saw free speech as a complicated instrument of power. He argued that discourse invariably reflects societal power structures and asserted that those who control dialogue ultimately control knowledge and truth. Therefore, free speech isn't merely a benign tool for individual expression; it can also mask and perpetuate power imbalances.

Thus, free speech isn't a black-and-white concept. It's a rich, vibrant, and complex tapestry woven from philosophical debates, ethical questions, historical happenstances, and societal norms. While some see free speech as a beacon of truth and an emblem of individuality, others worry about its potential to perpetuate unequal power dynamics.

Moreover, the philosophical explorations of free speech warrant new ponderings in the era of burgeoning digital communication. The advent of social media platforms has considerably altered the discourse around free speech. The digital sphere has massively increased the potential reach of every individual's speech, far surpassing the scale of any previous public forum. Consequently, the balance between respecting individual speeches and maintaining societal stability has become more intricate.

Additionally, the ability to spread misinformation or disinformation and the potential for digital platforms to be co-opted by nefarious forces pose new ethical implications to consider. As unprecedented digital advances fundamentally transform how we communicate, the philosophical understanding of free speech keeps evolving.

In conclusion, despite the complexities and diverging views, the fundamental philosophical underpinnings of free speech remain. It engenders the pursuit of truth, the right to personal and societal self-expression, and the equal treatment of all citizens. As society changes and evolves, so too does our understanding and analysis of free speech.

While discerning the philosophical, ethical, and societal implications of free speech is challenging, doing so provides us with pivotal insights. To defend, uphold, and when necessary, refashion these principles for a new generation, we must first deeply comprehend this complex, philosophical terrain.

As democratic citizens, it behooves us to grapple with these philosophical backgrounds, irrespective of how complex they might be. For it's through understanding the intricate, philosophical framework of free speech, we navigate the challenges and opportunities it presents. Even in the face of these complexities, we should endeavor to strike a balance that upholds the foundational principles without sacrificing societal harmony and progress.

Tolerance vs. Limitation: Seeking Balance

As we delve deeper into the nuances of free speech, it's essential to understand the delicate balance between tolerance of differing views and the necessary limitations to preserve public order. We find ourselves effectively on a high wire, striving to maintain a balance that protects our democratic ideals while simultaneously ensuring that our society is safe from dangerous or damaging expressions.

The principle of tolerance is a cornerstone of American democracy; it's the ethos that permits a multitude of ideas and perspectives to thrive. However, like any democratic principle, it's not without its limitations. It's these limitations - important as they are - that create difficult, albeit necessary, paradoxes.

The tolerance paradox, as it's often called, posits that for a tolerant society to remain so, it must be intolerant of intolerance. In practicality, this relates to the need to limit speech that infringes upon the safety and rights of others. Speech that can incite violence or create a hostile environment could feasibly fall into this category.

Recognizing such limitations reaffirms the notion that freedom of speech isn't an absolute right. There's a delicate balance at play which acknowledges the need for a breadth of ideas, including those that challenge or disturb us, while also ensuring that certain forms of speech that may be harmful or dangerous can't thrive unchecked.

It may seem a complex task to balance tolerance and limitation effectively in matters of free speech. But it's imperative we remember what's at stake. Too much limitation could result in a chilling effect, stifling free thought and democratic dialogue, while too much tolerance could potentially foster a harmful or hostile environment.

In striking this balance, it's crucial to consider context. Not all speech has the same potential impact. An inflammatory comment online might not hold the same potential threat as a direct, verbal threat to an individual in person. Knowing this, we need to look at the context in which the speech happens, the intent behind the statement, and its potential harm.

Equally important to context is the distinction between public and private speech. There's an assumption that public speech, due to its potential wider-reaching impact, might require closer regulation than private speech.

Still, it's worth noting that this dichotomy isn't entirely accurate. Sometimes, private speech can morph into public speech, as when something confidential is shared on social media. The fluidity between these two spaces only further highlights the complexity in striking a balance in issues of free speech.

Another aspect to consider in this balancing act is cultural relativity. Remember, what we deem tolerable or intolerable is often heavily impacted by cultural norms and values. For instance, in a society that heavily values individual rights, speech violating the rights of others may see tighter limitations. It's essential in this pursuit of balance that we remain mindful of the cultural-specific context of speech.

Throughout this discourse, we must never lose sight of the reason behind both tolerance and limitation. The heightening of discourse, the fostering of varied viewpoints, and a thriving marketplace for ideas are intrinsic to the beauty of free speech, while maintaining a secure environment devoid of hate speech or incitement, keeps our society safe.

In wrestling with these concepts of tolerance and limitation, we grapple with a quintessential dilemma of democratic society: how do we uphold freedom while protecting individuals from potential harm, both physical and psychological? It's a question without a definitive answer, instead requiring constant vigilance, iteration, and refinement.

Ultimately, the struggle to balance tolerance with limitation in matters of free speech remains an ongoing challenge in American society. However, despite its inherent complexities and difficulties, it is a challenge we must welcome. For, at the end of the day, it's through this struggle that we gain a richer understanding of our own commitment to free expression, democracy, and the dignity of all individuals.

So, as we continue forward, we must retain our awareness of diverging voices and perspectives, never losing sight of their importance. Yet, we must remain equally cognizant of the need to limit certain forms of speech that could harm or threaten others. It's a difficult line to walk, but a necessary path in our continual pursuit of a free, just, and democratic society.

In short, our task is to respect the spirit of free expression while also taking the necessary measures to prevent the platform from being used as a tool for harm. Yes, it's a challenge. But it's through these trials that we define and redefine the essence of our democratic society, while still safeguarding the principles on which the First Amendment was founded.

When Private Entities Censor: Responsibilities and Dilemmas

In the journey to understand the intriguing contours of free speech, we've been eyeing government restrictions, societal boundaries, and ethical quandaries. Now, let's shift our gaze towards the giant corporations that increasingly wield power over our public discourse. As we know, the First Amendment's speech protections predominantly apply to government actions. But, what happens when private entities like social media platforms and corporations decide to restrict certain speech or expressions?

One of the crucial dilemmas of our digital world arises from the fact that the public squares once operated by governments have largely been superseded by privately owned online platforms. Tech giants like Twitter, Facebook, and Google significantly influence public discourse, with their decisions about content moderation often instigating widespread debate. This prominence begs the question - what is their responsibility towards free speech, and how does their meddling influence it?

On one hand, these platforms, as private entities, have commercial rights to set rules for their user communities and to protect their own interests. They're not bound by the First Amendment that primarily guards against government abuses. They can, and do, have rules that restrict certain types of content in order to foster safe and welcoming environments for their users. The exceptions they make for violent speech, nudity, hate speech, and more are seen as necessary trade-offs.

However, when these same private entities become too enthusiastic about censors, their influence can resemble the power of the state over speech. They control what millions of people see, read, and discuss daily. Their influence stretches far beyond American shores, impacting global discourse. The wielders of this control, quite reasonably, face questions of transparency, accountability, and arbitrariness.

Let's consider an example. In early 2021, major social media platforms, including Twitter and Facebook, decided to banish then-President Donald Trump from their platforms citing repeated policy violations. A number of private entities made a collective decision that affected public speech, causing a heated debate over censorship, free speech, and the power that private entities wield over it

Detractors argued that this was an instance of unrestrained corporate power censoring political speech. Advocates countered that private entities were exercising their rights to conduct their businesses as they deemed fit, imposing restrictions to prevent harmful behavior. Both perspectives highlight crucial issues in the ongoing dialogue about private entities and censorship.

A key piece of the puzzle is Section 230 of the Communications Decency Act, a federal law that's crucial for understanding the responsibilities and protections of these platforms. It allows these online services to remove user-generated content that violates their policies without being deemed the speaker or publisher of the content, and protects them from liability for a broad swath of content posted by users.

Some argue that the protection offered by Section 230 should come with higher accountability and transparency from these platforms. They contend that these entities shouldn't have unchecked control over public discourse. Others counter that imposing additional obligations on platforms would stifle innovation, compel them to over-censor out of an abundance of caution, and potentially infringe on their own free speech rights.

It's also worth noting that many critics of censorship by private entities aren't demanding complete freedom from rules. They're asking for more clarity and consistency in the application of those rules. Users being banned without understanding why, or controversial figures being allowed to keep disseminating offensive content, fosters frustration, confusion, and mistrust among users.

Moreover, the issue isn't limited to the tech realm. Traditional companies and corporations extend their influence over speech through their advertising choices and commercial policies. For instance, companies pulling their advertisements from a particular program or network can effectively exert pressure on the kind of speech tolerated on those platforms.

In essence, when private entities censor, objectives often clash. The desire for a safe, welcoming space clashes with the push for unhampered dialogue. Commercial interests rub up against public good. Consistency, transparency, accountability, and fairness take center stage in these discussions.

While this predicament doesn't have an easy or one-size-fits-all solution, engaging in informed discourse can lead to improved practices and policy changes over time. The role of private entities in the arena of free speech is a complex and nuanced issue. Coming to grips with the layers of this issue is essential to grasp the larger picture of free speech in today's age.

The tensions stemming from the role private entities play in moderating speech are not necessarily indicative of a broken system. Rather, they reaffirm the need for continual review, necessitating that we stay engaged, educated, and involved in this crucial dialogue. The free exchange of ideas depends on it.

Global Perspectives: How the U.S. Compares Internationally

As we venture into this global perspective of free speech rights, it's valuable to remember that the United States doesn't exist in a vacuum. Amidst diverse cultures, established political systems, and unique histories, the freedom of speech holds a distinctive status in different parts of the world. It's essential to dive into these perspectives to broaden our understanding of this fundamental human right.

First and foremost, let's compare the U.S. to its nearby neighbor, Canada. Although both nations are based on the principles of democracy and free speech, their legal iteration of these values isn't identical. Unlike the U.S., where hate speech can potentially enjoy the protection of the First Amendment, Canada has adopted a more restrictive approach. Canada's Charter of Rights and Freedoms allows the government to place reasonable limitations on speech deemed to incite hate against any identifiable group.

Moving across the Atlantic Ocean, the European Union showcases an array of perspectives on free speech. The European Convention on Human Rights guarantees freedom of expression but also accentuates the responsibilities and penalties that come with it. Member states can restrict speech to maintain the authority of the judiciary, protect health or morals and prevent the disclosure of information received in confidence.

In a French context, free speech is protected under the Declaration of the Rights of Man and Citizen of 1789. However, like Canada, France imposes restrictions on hate speech and has even outlawed denial of the Holocaust. Similarly, Germany, scarred by its Nazi past, has strict laws against hate speech and any glorification of the Nazi regime.

Contrastingly, Nordic countries like Denmark and Norway are often seen as bastions of free speech, with their legal norms showing tolerance towards a wider band of expressive behavior than many other European nations.

Traveling to the Eastern part of the globe, countries like China and North Korea present a stark contrast to the Western values of free speech. Authoritarian regimes control and suppress dissenting voices, exhibiting little tolerance for free speech.

We also find countries where the divide between citizens' perspectives and the law creates an interesting dynamic. In India, the world's largest democracy, free speech is constitutionally protected but is subjected to "reasonable restrictions." These restrictions, often criticized for being far-reaching, can limit discourse. Yet, despite the legal constraints, India's vibrant civil society continues to push boundaries and debate freely in many spaces.

In Japan, the freedom of speech is safeguarded by Article 21 of their constitution. Yet, the society's ingrained emphasis on harmony often discourages outspoken criticism or dissent. Meanwhile, Russia, ostensibly a democracy, is often criticized for its veiled suppression of free speech, dissent, and protest under the guise of protecting societal stability and security.

In Africa, free speech freedom varies widely across the continent. South Africa, for instance, has strong constitutional protections for freedom of speech compared to countries like Eritrea, widely considered one of the world's most censored countries.

In Latin America, Brazil, with its strong democratic constitution, protects free expression. However, concerns have been raised about threats to this freedom in recent years. Conversely, Venezuela has been pointed out for aggressive control and suppression of the media.

As we sail the seas of worldwide free speech norms, it's evident that every nation is unique. Each country's legal, political, and social context affects how free speech is protected and defined. The comparison isn't about judging based on a superior/inferior binary but understanding the complexity and diversity in the global dialogue on free speech.

Understanding these global perspectives on free speech not only broadens our viewpoint but also helps us better appreciate and question our system. Amidst this vibrant global mosaic, the U.S. possesses a noteworthy place, with its world-renowned protection of speech. However, this worldwide journey is an invitation to question norms, to challenge our understanding, and to open doors to new perspectives.

In the end, this venture compels us to reflect on a critical question: What is the true meaning of free speech, and how best can it be protected, nurtured, and responsibly exercised? The next stage of our journey will shed light on these questions, as we circle back to our home turf and contemplate the challenges and considerations lying ahead for free speech in the U.S.

Chapter 6:
The Road Ahead: Challenges and Considerations for the Future

The challenges of the future in relation to free speech set a complex tableau that we must comprehend if we are not to stand immobile, beset by insurmountable obstacles. On one hand, burgeoning technology has irreversibly shaped the speech landscape, carving out spaces for instantaneous global dialogues that our legislation struggles to comprehend, let alone regulate. With the internet acting as a digital Wild West for speech acts, we're in the unenviable position of regulating a frontier we can't fully visualize. Concurrent with this, there's an ongoing struggle in striking a workable equilibrium between our national security and cherished personal freedoms. This critical issue is further complicated by shifting geopolitical dynamics and the persistent yet nebulous threat of terrorism. Thus, delineating legitimate security measures from clandestine incursions on personal expression poses a significant quandary. Lastly, our road cannot be traveled without considering the role of education in fostering informed expression. We often forget that free speech is as much about listening and understanding as it is about speaking. The capacity to discern fact from fabrication, to evaluate claims and sources critically, is an indispensable cornerstone of functional, responsible free speech. Stepping upon this complex path, we must be prepared for daunting yet necessary negotiations of our collective understanding of free speech.

Technology's Role in Shaping the Speech Landscape

In the ever-evolving arena of communication, no other factor has transformed the landscape of speech quite like technology. Be it social media, machine learning algorithms, or the shift from print to digital platforms, the symbiotic relationship between technology and freedom of speech is one that cannot be overlooked.

Technology has been a boon for free speech. In essence, it has made voice democratization a reality. With the Internet, anyone with a connection can share their thoughts and ideas with the world. No longer are we solely dependent on traditional media outlets – newspapers, television, and radio – to disseminate information. Social media platforms, blogs, and websites have provided all of us with the tools to become publishers in our own right.

However, the proliferation of speech through digital channels has also led to new challenges. The scale at which information spreads online has made it increasingly difficult to separate fact from fiction. Disinformation campaigns, deep fake videos, and fake news are just a few examples of the potential misuse of free speech turned malignant, made vastly potent by technology.

Another challenge technology poses for free speech is the issue of censorship and moderation. Big Tech companies like Facebook, Twitter, and Google all have the power to moderate content on their platforms. While they have a responsibility to purge harmful content from their platforms, questions about consistency, transparency, and potential bias in their moderation practices introduce another layer of complexity to the free speech debate.

Apart from censorship and information quality, there's also the matter of privacy. People's right to express their ideas freely is oftentimes contingent upon their assurance of anonymity. Whistleblowers, activists, and even ordinary citizens rely on secure technological channels to communicate sensitive information. Ever-advancing surveillance tech and data breaches can impede this free flow of information.

The rise of artificial intelligence and machine learning raises additional questions about free speech. Algorithms that help social media platforms detect harmful content can help maintain a healthier digital ecosystem. However, these same algorithms could suppress certain perspectives and inadvertently violate the principles of free speech.

Further, technology has expanded the battlefront for free speech to the realm of cybercrime. Instances of online harassment, doxing, and cyberbullying have highlighted the darker side of digital communication. Here, the complexities of legal jurisdiction and international cooperation add to the challenge of promoting free speech while curbing misuse.

Even seemingly innocuous technological features like autocomplete suggestions or personalized content feeds can have a profound impact on free speech. These underlying algorithms can reinforce our existing beliefs and insulate us from diverse perspectives, leading to the phenomenon known as 'echo chambers' or 'filter bubbles'.

It's also worth noting how technology is shaping speech beyond the domain of social media and the Internet. Advances in areas like virtual and augmented reality are starting to redefine our understanding of shared and public spaces, which are vital pillars for free speech. How we legislate for free speech in these burgeoning digital realms will be a key question for the future.

The role of technology in shaping the speech landscape is a broad and challenging topic. While it's clear that tech has enfranchised millions and given a global platform to voices that would traditionally have been marginalized, it's also evident that it's introduced a new set of complex challenges that our legal system must find ways to address.

As we navigate this evolving speech landscape, the decisions we make today about moderation, algorithmic transparency, privacy protections, and legal regulation will profoundly shape the future of free speech. Technology can be a powerful tool for amplifying and protecting free speech, but we must ensure it's wielded responsibly.

While technology continues to present challenges to free speech, it's important to remember that it also offers solutions. Tools for anonymous browsing or encrypted communication can protect those who need to express themselves without fear of retribution. Artificial intelligence can help us combat harmful content, and transparency initiatives can hold big tech accountable for preserving the principle of free speech.

The symbiosis between technology and free speech will continue to define our public discourse. As technology evolves, so too must our understanding and framework of free speech. It's up to us to harness technology's potential for good while mitigating its capacity for harm, maintaining the delicate balance that makes free speech not only a constitutional right, but a cornerstone of our democracy.

As we venture even deeper into the digital age, it's ever more apparent that our approach toward bridging technology and free speech must be both flexible and firm. Advancements in technology offer us an opportunity to rethink and maybe even redefine what free speech means for our generation and the ones that follow.

Balancing National Security and Personal Freedoms

The delicate balance between national security and personal freedoms is an enduring subject at the heart of First Amendment debates. It's a tightrope walk, balancing the necessary security measures required to protect a nation and its citizens, with the preservation of individual liberties, a hallmark of democracy.

National security often demands regulations, controls, and surveillance as a measure to protect and preserve the nation and its people. In the wake of horrific events such as 9/11, the Boston Marathon bombing, and the increase in cyber warfare, the government's role in preserving national security has become more demanding. Comprehensive and sometimes invasive security measures are frequently justified in the name of public safety.

This somewhat understandable reach into personal freedoms, however, encroaches on the very liberties democracy is designed to protect. Among these is the First Amendment right to free speech, a cornerstone of personal freedom and democratic governance.

Unrestrained free speech can sometimes pose a challenge to national security. For example, the diversification of media platforms has given rise to groups using these platforms to propagate hate speech, sow division, and incite violence. In such instances, the government is obliged to intervene, but these interventions often lead to debates around censorship and government overreach.

The question becomes: where does a government draw the line between protecting national security and infringing upon personal freedoms? It's a difficult calculus with no easy answers, owed in part to the dynamic nature of each concept. National security threats evolve with the global landscape, while societal views of what qualifies as an infringing upon free speech also shift over time.

In the digital age, balancing these two equally important concepts becomes even more challenging. Vast amounts of information are shared daily on the internet, and it's a herculean task to monitor and govern this space without encroaching too much on individual freedoms.

Take, for example, the infamous Snowden revelation that revealed an extensive surveillance program by the National Security Agency (NSA). The program led to a heated debate about whether such surveillance infringed on personal freedoms. Ultimately, a balance was sought between allowing the NSA to continue its programs in the interest of national security, and holding the agency accountable for its surveillance practices to uphold citizens' rights to privacy.

In the realm of social and digital media, the question of balance grows even more complex. The expansion of these platforms has been accompanied by an increase in disinformation campaigns and cyber attacks, both of which pose significant threats to national security. Meanwhile, the attempt to regulate these channels raises pained questions about censorship and restriction of personal freedoms.

It is essential to understand that with every gain in national security measures - be it through surveillance, monitoring or regulation - there's a corresponding potential loss of personal freedom. It's a trade-off that requires persistent scrutiny and adjustment, always with the aim of maximizing both parameters.

At the heart of this delicate balance lies the rule of law. Both national security and free speech must abide by the law, and where laws may infringe upon personal freedoms, the courts have a crucial role to play in reestablishing equilibrium.

The courts are not infallible, of course. They too grapple with difficult choices, and their decisions sometimes face critique. However, the judicial system, in the ongoing interpretation of the First Amendment, plays a vital role in maintaining the fragile equilibrium between national security and personal freedoms.

Through it all, everyone - the government, the judiciary, and society at large - must remember the fundamental principles that guide these debates: equality, freedom, and democracy. National security must not be a guise for curbing democratic freedoms, and free speech rights must not tip over into anarchy or lawlessness.

The duty to balance national security and personal freedoms belongs to all of us. It's not just about the laws we enact or the court decisions we support, but the public discourse we engage in and the values we uphold as a society. It's a balancing act that, when performed with informed, conscientious and vigilant participation, fortifies the very foundation of our democracy.

The Role of Education in Fostering Informed Expression

Delving into the power of education, we find its paramount role in shaping society. Education is the wind that fills the sails of enlightenment, guiding the ship of progress. In no sphere is the role of education more critical than in promoting informed expression. In essence, effective education equips students with the tools to engage in meaningful, persuasive, and factually accurate communication, supporting the functionality of a robust democracy.

The foundation of any discourse, particularly public discourse, is information. An educational system that prioritizes critical thinking, media literacy, and the ability to assess and validate information, fosters a populace capable of engaging in substantive, informed expression. This becomes increasingly essential as society navigates currents of misinformation, biased narratives, and divisive rhetoric, often amplified by technology and social media platforms.

There's a common misconception that education's role in this context is merely to fill students' minds with information. However, that's only part of the picture. In a world where digital technology has made information ubiquitous, the ability to sift through, analyze, and interpret that information becomes much more valuable. The cultivation of these skills bears a critical influence on the capacity for informed expression.

Take, for example, the need for media literacy. Given today's landscape where technological sophistication can make falsehoods appear deceptively authentic, the education system holds the mantle for equipping the youth with the tools to distinguish fact from fiction, propaganda from journalism. When citizens can critically evaluate the credibility of sources and challenge information that is served to them, they become a part of a discourse that is truly informed.

In addition to teaching media literacy, the process of discerning the value of various sources of information needs to be instilled in students. Informed expression isn't just about having information, but about understanding the source of that information, its credibility, and the bias it may carry. This discernment facilitates more nuanced debates, richer political discussions, and reasoned decision-making.

Educational institutions possess an indispensable task in fostering informed expression in areas that are often difficult to navigate. These could be contentious subjects like religion, race or political ideology. By fostering an atmosphere of respectful debate, they can encourage students to express their views without fear of reprisal, and in turn, learn to listen and respond to opposing viewpoints with understanding rather than antagonism.

Credentials alone doesn't forge informed citizens. It is a blend of knowledge, skills, and attitude. For instance, having data on income inequality isn't the same as comprehending the complexities of economic policies or the societal impacts of these inequalities. Therefore, an education system that encourages critical thinking, inquiry, and empathy is crucial in breeding informed expression.

Another salient reason education is paramount in fostering informed expression is its ability to shape tomorrow's leaders, journalists, entrepreneurs, teachers, and voters, by instilling in them the importance of ethical communications. Part of informed expression comes from understanding the power words carry and the consequences they can have on individuals and society. Teaching the principles of ethics in communications ensures our future communicators understand the weight of their words.

An informed citizen can question, can challenge, and can drive change. Education should not be about binary oppositions of "right" or "wrong" answers, but about encouraging facets of uncertainty, greyness and ambiguity. Cultivating informed expression requires fostering a willingness to deal with uncertainty, teaching the skills to untangle complexities and generate clarity.

Debates, group discussions and presentations, research papers and essays should replace rote memorization and regurgitation of textbook content.

Understanding global cultural and societal nuances also underscores the role of education in fostering informed expression. We must recognize that expressing an informed opinion doesn't exist in a vacuum. As our societies become more multicultural and interconnected, the ability to understand and navigate the cultural subtleties becomes essential. This empathy helps to prevent misunderstandings, hostility, and fosters a more harmonious society.

It's undeniable that nurturing informed expression demands a shift from traditional pedagogical methods. A paradigm shift to more thought-provoking, dialogue-inciting, and problem-solving oriented education could be the change we need. As educators, we need to inspire curiosity, spark a desire for learning, and promote respect for diverse perspectives.

In conclusion, the role of education in fostering informed expression is paramount, forming the bedrock of democratic societies. By equipping individuals with the tools to critically evaluate information, delineate fact from fiction, and to express and respect diverse views with understanding and empathy, the education system can and should serve as the scaffold upon which informed expression rests.

Refining our education system to better foster informed expression won't be a quick or easy process, but the stakes are too high not to try. The successful implementation of this cultivation of informed expression transcends beyond the individual to the collective, forming the fabric of our society - a society that is informed, resilient and capable of fostering constructive dialogue.

Conclusion:
The Ever-Evolving Wall of Words:
Our Collective Responsibility

We've taken quite a journey through the untamed terrain of free speech, its challenges, contours, potential pitfalls, and shining promises, and we stand now at the concluding chapter of this odyssey. We've understood the Founding Father's creative intellect through the First Amendment, analyzed landmark cases, delved into the medium's censorship, and discerned when speech becomes a crime.

At this juncture, it's worth stating that free speech isn't a static ideal firmly etched into our collective ethos. It's a living, breathing concept, always in flux, shaped by our experiences and challenges. We should anticipate change, not fear it, for within it lies the opportunity to adapt and ensure that the highest ideals of free speech are upheld.

Such change isn't just driven by law or institutional measures. It's driven by societal shifts, opinions, cultural sensibilities, and technological advancements. It's incumbent upon us, as a society, to make crucial judgments about acceptable speech and its limits, balancing equitable expression with the need to curtail harmful rhetoric.

The advent of the digital era has revolutionized our communication landscape, inviting new debates regarding online discourse and personal freedoms. We must grapple with technology's role in shaping the 'Wall of Words', assess its benefits whilst mitigating its pitfalls. Herein, we embrace our shared responsibility to mindfully negotiate these slippery paths and channel online discourse towards constructive aims, promoting understanding and nuance in an increasingly polarized world.

As a pluralistic society, America is a rich tapestry of diverse cultures, religions, and philosophies. The conversations triggered by this diversity can be uncomfortable, even confrontational, but they are integral to a healthy democracy. They challenge our preconceived notions, push us outside our comfort zones, and ultimately usher in greater understanding and compassion.

A balance must be struck between tolerance and limitation. Tolerance allows all voices to be represented in the public square, but without appropriate limitations, it's trivially easy for malevolent entities to exploit tolerance in service of divise, hateful ideologies. Informing this balance is a crucial part of ensuring the health and vibrancy of our democracy.

Private entities, especially social media platforms, play an increasingly consequential role in this narrative. They inevitably find themselves faced with moral and ethical dilemmas regarding what content to permit, limit, or ban outright. These entities bear a tremendous responsibility, and they need to conduct themselves with transparency, accountability, and a commitment to the essential principles of free speech.

We must not lose sight of the global context in this discourse. Just as we learn from the international community, our actions resonate beyond our borders. We must uphold the highest standards of free speech, not just for our benefit, but as part of our obligation to promote liberty and free expression worldwide.

Education plays a vital role in nurturing a generation of informed, thoughtful communicators who understand the responsibilities, ethical implications, and social impact accompanying the right to free speech. It prepares us to deal rationally and civilly, avoiding the pitfalls of reactionary rhetoric, disinformation and false narratives.

Amidst this dynamic landscape of free speech, it's we, the people, who construct the 'Wall of Words', brick by brick. Each word we utter, every viewpoint we express, shapes this structure and determines whether it serves as a beacon of free, respectful discourse or an insurmountable barrier of hate, division, and misunderstanding.

Our collective responsibility, then, is to use the power of speech as a tool of understanding, reconciliation, and progress. This does not mean silencing discordant notes in the symphony of voices. On the contrary, it means taking the effort to comprehend the essence of these voices and encouraging a discussion grounded in respect and empathy.

And so, as we have journeyed together through the complexities of free speech, remember that the purpose of this voyage wasn't just to inform but to inspire. Let's keep investing our thoughts, words, and actions to further the core values our Founding Fathers established to encourage understanding, tolerance, and respect for plurality, even as we construct, deconstruct, and reconstruct the 'Ever-Evolving Wall of Words'.

Our freedom of speech – its defense, its exercise, its constraints, and yes, its controversies – stand not apart from us, but reflect who we are as a society. And who we can be.

In conclusion, may we work tirelessly in our collective endeavor to uphold, refine, and expand the arenas for free speech, thus paving the way for an enriched, empathetic, and empowering democratic discourse.

Appendix A: Glossary of Legal and Media Terms

The following glossary aims to provide clear definitions and explanations for the legal and media terms used throughout this book.

- **Blackmail:** Illegally forcing someone to act against their will using threats, often to expose information that would harm their reputation or relationships.
- **Censorship:** The official prohibition or restriction of any type of expression believed to violate common standards of decency, pose a threat to public safety, or challenge the power of the state.
- **Commercial Speech:** Communication, like advertising, that seeks to promote a commercial transaction. While protected by the First Amendment, it does not enjoy the same degree of protection as other types of speech.
- **Conspiracy:** An agreement between two or more persons to commit an illegal act, or a legal act in an illegal way, whether it occurs or not.
- **Contempt of Court:** Behavior that disrespects or obstructs the functioning of the court, including disobedience of court orders or disrespectful behavior during court proceedings.
- **Copyright Infringement:** Using, selling, or copying someone else's copyrighted work without permission.
- **Cyberbullying:** Unwanted and aggressive behavior toward others using electronic or digital means, including social networks, email, and text messages.
- **Defamation:** A false statement, presented as a fact, that injures someone's reputation. This is divided into slander

(spoken defamation) and libel (written or broadcast defamation).

- **Doxing:** The internet-based practice of researching and publicizing personally identifiable or confidential information about an individual.
- **Disclosure of Classified Information:** The act of revealing classified or sensitive information without appropriate authorization, known colloquially as "leaking."
- **Extortion:** The act of obtaining something, particularly money, through force or threats.
- **False Advertising:** The use of misleading or factually inaccurate statements in advertising.
- **False Reports:** Providing untrue information with the intent to mislead, particularly in legal or media contexts.
- **Fighting Words:** Speech intended to incite violence or disturbance of the peace. This kind of speech is not protected by the First Amendment.
- **Fraud:** Intentional deception to secure unfair or unlawful gain, or to deprive a victim of a legal right.
- **Hate Speech:** Communication that offends, threatens, or insults groups, based on characteristics such as race, color, religion, national origin, sexual orientation, or other traits.
- **Harassment:** Unsolicited words or actions intended to annoy, threaten, or intimidate another person or group.
- **Incitement:** Encouraging or stirring up violent or unlawful behavior.
- **Obscenity:** Expression, particularly in speech or print, that offends the prevalent morality or decency of the time, and lacks artistic or scientific value.
- **Perjury:** Lying under oath during a legal proceeding. It is a crime because it undermines the function of courts and inquiries.
- **Regulated Industries:** Sectors of the economy, such as healthcare and banking, that are directly controlled by government authorities.
- **Restraining Orders/Protective Orders:** Legal orders issued by a court to protect a person(s) from being harmed or harassed by another person(s).

- **Solicitation of a Crime:** One person's act of encouraging, requesting, or commanding another to commit a crime.
- **Trade Secrets:** A company's confidential business information including designs, strategies, and practices, which provide it with a competitive advantage.
- **True Threats:** Statements where the speaker means to communicate a serious expression of an intent to commit an act of unlawful violence.

Appendix B:
Landmark Cases Briefs

In this section, we take a concentrated look at some of the most influential cases that have helped shape the boundaries of free speech in America. These are summaries of complex legal stories, presented with the intent to provide a fundamental understanding of key principles and their real-world applications.

Schenck v. United States (1919)

In this early landmark case, the Supreme Court established the "clear and present danger" test to determine restrictions on speech. Charles Schenck mailed pamphlets urging resistance to the draft during World War I. He was charged with violating the Espionage Act. The Court held that Schenck's speech created a clear and present danger that brought about "substantive evils" the government had a right to prevent. This set a precedent for restrictions when speech poses a real, immediate danger.

Near v. Minnesota (1931)

This case established the principle of no prior restraint, holding it unconstitutional for a law to provide government censorship of the press in most situations. Jay M. Near published scandalous accusations against local officials. Minnesota officials sought to halt publication under a state law. The Court struck down the law, extending First Amendment protections for the press against most forms of prior restraint.

Brandenburg v. Ohio (1969)

Brandenburg, a Ku Klux Klan leader, was prosecuted under an Ohio law for inciting violence at a Klan rally. The Supreme Court overturned his conviction, creating the "imminent lawless action" test. It held that for advocacy to amount to incitement, it must be directed to inciting or producing imminent lawless action and be likely to produce such action. Brandenburg v. Ohio extended significant protection to inflammatory speech.

Miller v. California (1973)

A key case on obscenity, Marvin Miller mailed explicit materials promoting adult books and films. He was convicted under a California statute mimicking Obscenity Law. The Court upheld the conviction, producing the "Miller Test" to define obscenity: (a) whether the average person, applying contemporary community standards, would find that the work appeals to the prurient interest; (b) whether the work depicts or describes, in a patently offensive manner, sexual conduct; (c) whether the work, taken as a whole, lacks serious literary, artistic, political, or scientific value.

Texas v. Johnson (1989)

This case emerged when Gregory Johnson burned a U.S. flag in Dallas during a political demonstration and was convicted under a Texas statute. The Court held that Johnson's burning of the flag was expressive conduct protected by the First Amendment. This decision confirmed that symbolic speech can have the same protections as verbal speech.

Reno v. ACLU (1997)

A milestone in internet regulation, this case challenged the Communications Decency Act of 1996 which sought to protect minors from harmful material online. In a unanimous decision, the Supreme Court struck down the law, holding it overly broad and a violation of freedom of expression. This cemented the principle that internet speech deserves at least as much First Amendment protection as speech in print.

Each of these cases highlights important aspects of how free speech has been interpreted and reinterpreted over time, surely confirming that free speech is a living concept, ever evolving with the societal norms, technologies, and challenges.